# HIGH-PERFORMANCE FACILITIES MANAGEMENT

### A Guide
### for
### Total Workplace Design and Management

## DAN BRATHAL, B.A.

### AND

## DR. MARK LANGEMO, CRM

# HIGH-PERFORMANCE FACILITIES MANAGEMENT

Doug —

Best Wishes,

Dan Brathal

# Comments About This Book

"Through my relationship with Dan Brathal and through our joint participation in leadership roles within IFMA, I have come to know him as a progressive, forward-thinking professional business manager. This book has captured the essence and ultimate purpose of Facilities Management—integration of workplace design and management that enables an organization to be competitive and achieve their business goals. Dan and Mark have provided a comprehensive overview of the components and methods to achieve the total workplace."

*Roger P. McCombs*
*Vice President, Business Shared Services*
*Medtronic, Inc.*
*Minneapolis, Minnesota*

"You asked me for comments about your new book. I think you have covered the bases you needed to cover and covered them well. These areas are integral parts of most facilities managers' lives. I also think the inclusion of examples and techniques increases the richness of the book."

*Richard Palmer, President*
*Palmer Consulting (Facilities Management)*
*Maple Grove, Minnesota*

"Having known and worked with Dan Brathal for over 30 years, the last several years of my career with Dan reporting directly to me as Manager of 3M's Facilities Management operation, I have witnessed his increasingly strong understanding of totally integrated workplace design and management. I have also known Dr. Langemo for nearly 25 years and I am familiar with his very positive reputation as an educator, consultant, speaker, author, and leader in the fields of workplace development and information management. I believe everyone involved with facilities management, architecture, engineering, interior design, information management, administrative services, and other components of workplace design and management will benefit from reading this book."

*James R. Jensen*
*Retired VP, Office Administration*
*3M Company*
*Burnet, Texas*

"I had the privilege of working with Dan Brathal and Mark Langemo years ago. Reading portions of this new book made me want to go back to work.....well, almost! That's a lie because I like what I'm doing now—not working! But, this is a good book. You will enjoy it and learn from it."

*William V. Nygren*
*Retired Manager, Office Services*
*3M Company*
*Mesa, Arizona*

# HIGH-PERFORMANCE FACILITIES MANAGEMENT

## A Guide
## for
## Total Workplace Design and Management

## Daniel A. Brathal, B.A.
### and
## Dr. Mark Langemo, CRM

Knight Printing
Grand Forks, North Dakota

This book is dedicated to:

## Jacque Brathal

## and

## Diane Langemo

## Steve Langemo, Brent Voeller, Darrin Voeller

"This publication is designed to provide accurate and authoritative information in regard to the subject matter covered. It is sold with the understanding that the publisher and authors are not engaged in rendering legal, accounting or other professional service. If legal advice or other expert assistance is required, the services of a competent professional person should be sought." Excerpt from the Declaration of Principles jointly adopted by a Committee of the American Bar Association and a Committee of Publishers and Associations.

Knight Printing
5203 Gateway Drive
Grand Forks, ND  58203
Phone: 701-746-4543
Fax: 701-746-0944

Cover Design:  Knight Printing

Printed in the United States of America
2004

ISBN: 0-9747143-0-5

# CONTENTS

# Chapter 4:                         43

## Components of High-Performance Facilities Management Programs

# Chapter 5:                         63

## Assessing Your Organization's Current Facilities Management Situation

# Chapter 6:                         75

## Winning Strategies for High-Performance Facilities Management

# Chapter 7:       91

## Office Layout and Design:  Experienced Insights

# Chapter 8:       109

## Roles of Facilities Management in Health, Safety, and Environment

# Chapter 9:       119

## Facilities Planning for Information and Technology Systems

# Chapter 10:                                                     135
## Facilities Management and Records Management: A Partnership

# Chapter 11:                                                     157
## Potential and Challenges of Telecommuting

# Chapter 12:                                                     165
## Assuring Business Continuity and Resumption

# Chapter 13: 183
## Roles of Suppliers in High-Performance Facilities Management

# Chapter 14: 189
## Managing and Motivating Facilities Management Personnel

# Chapter 15: 205
## Resources for Facilities Managers

# Foreword

People need places in which to live and work. For the vast majority of people, the places in which they live and the workplaces they develop or are employed to inhabit will be facilities—buildings and structures—of some type. Those structures and buildings and facilities will not manage themselves. What will always be needed will be individuals charged with responsibilities for conceiving, planning, designing, constructing, equipping, using, managing, and caring for those places for living or working. Hopefully, those individuals will consider themselves to be professionals in the true sense of the word. Hopefully, they will be continually striving to perform their facilities management responsibilities based on their state-of-the-art knowledge, competence, and caring commitments to accomplish high-performance facilities management.

It is refreshing to have a state-of-the-art and current-to-the-moment facilities management book that is not a textbook or a tedious manual. *High-Performance Facilities Management* is a practical guide for use in implementing or strengthening appropriate and comprehensive facilities management programs that will result in high-quality places for people to live and work.

In many organizations, especially smaller ones, facilities management has often been left more or less to chance. Unfortunately, in some companies or organizations, no one individual has been designated to really be the "facilities manager" and the facilities have often been left to more or less flounder. In other organizations or companies, individuals have been asked to be facilities managers but then have not been given the senior management support necessary to develop the expertise and knowledge required as a base for developing organization-wide facilities management programs. Perhaps management did not find facilities management issues as important as other aspects of organizational development and operation. More likely, they saw facilities management as a cost to the company's or organization's bottom line.

Fortunately, facilities management has evolved as a profession that now encompasses multiple disciplines interacting to develop, manage, and ensure that high-quality living and working environments will exist by integrating the best of people, places, processes, and technologies. Professional facilities managers are now routinely assigned wide ranges of responsibilities for planning, designing, and managing facilities. They are usually responsible for coordinating physical workplaces with the people and the work that needs to be accomplished for organizations to be successful, competitive, and profitable.

The body of knowledge required of facilities managers is extensive, complex, technologically sophisticated, and is increasing in scope every passing day. Facilities managers—like colleague professionals in medicine, law, or business—can never know enough and can always benefit from learning more. Integrating principles of architecture, administration, behavioral sciences, business administration, engineering, information systems, records management, human relations, professional management, and expertise from other disciplines requires a commitment to learning and continuing education. And, sometimes the most important learning is that gained not only through one's own experience but also through the shared experiences of industry veterans—others who have "walked in the same shoes" while covering the same ground.

In 2001 the United States experienced the terrorist attacks on the World Trade Center and on the Pentagon. In the aftermath of those terrible events, more business leaders and government leaders have become increasingly concerned about their facilities and their abilities to withstand potential disasters in order to continue availability as places for people to live and work. Facilities management continues to increase in stature and importance as a major concern of facility owners, business executives, government administrators, and leaders in all organizations. There are many human security, economic, financial, legal, competitive, and practical reasons for developing and managing appropriate facilities for living and for the successful futures of business, industry, and government.

With more and more leaders and people at all levels increasingly understanding and appreciating the need for high-quality facilities management, *High-Performance Facilities Management* offers tried-and-proven approaches and the practical advice needed to strengthen existing facilities management programs or to develop and implement new organization-wide programs. A facilities management program is neither a luxury nor an option. Facilities management programs are needed for purposes of coordinating the planning, design, development, implementation, use, and management of the buildings, structures, and other facilities used as spaces for living and for working. This book presents valuable insights about how to secure management support for and how to develop and manage organization-wide facilities management programs.

Daniel A. Brathal, B.A., is a recognized authority on facilities management. A veteran of nearly 33 years at the headquarters of 3M Company in St. Paul, Minnesota, Dan Brathal managed numerous disciplines including corporate facilities management, information management, business continuity planning, strategic planning, quality improvement, and other corporate service organizations. More specifically, Dan was 3M's Manager of Facility Management Services from 1984 through 1997. In that capacity, he had responsibilities for the planning, design, development, furnishing, maintenance, space allocation, personnel moves, and related functions for all of 3M's research and administrative facilities at the company's headquarters in St. Paul.

Dan Brathal was assigned in 1997 to the position of Manager, Corporate Site Management at 3M where he was responsible for Facilities Management Services, Records Management Services, Forms Management Services, Electronic Document Imaging, Custodial Services, Business Continuity Services, and Administrative Services Systems Support. Dan earned a B. A. degree (Summa Cum Laude) in Business Administration from Concordia University in St. Paul, Minnesota. He has been a leader in several professional associations including the International Facility Management Association (IFMA). He has co-authored three books and has delivered more than 75 executive and educational presentations at various universities, colleges, conventions, conferences and seminars throughout the United States and Canada. Dan Brathal has "been there and done that" with virtually every aspect of professional facilities management.

Now that the climate is right and the needs are greater than ever to establish successful facilities management programs or to strengthen existing ones, *High-Performance Facilities Management* and the expertise of Dan Brathal will help you succeed.

*Dr. Mark Langemo, CRM*
*University Business Professor Emeritus, Consultant, Author,*
*and Seminar Leader*

# Preface

*High-Performance Facilities Management* is written for people who are concerned about or are responsible for facilities management. It is crafted for people who need to know what facilities management is, what it should be, and why it is more critical to the success of individuals and organizations than ever before. This book was designed for those who need to know how to develop appropriate facilities management programs or strengthen existing programs and then enable them to work effectively and successfully on a day-in and day-out basis.

*High-Performance Facilities Management* is written for all those people who individually and collectively are repeatedly asking or are concerned about the following questions:

- ➡ What is facilities management today and what should it be tomorrow?

- ➡ Why is high-quality facilities management more important than ever in history?

- ➡ What is total workplace design and management?

- ➡ What should be included in high-performance facilities management programs?

- ➡ What will be the benefits to organizations if facilities programs are implemented?

- ➡ What strategies should be implemented to secure senior management support?

- ➡ What are the roles of architects in facilities management?

- ➡ What are the roles of engineers in facilities management?

- ➡ What are the roles of behavioral sciences in facilities management?

- ➡ How can roles of architecture, engineering, and behavioral sciences be integrated?

→ How can health concerns best be confronted and managed as part of facilities management?

→ How can good office layout and design principles be integrated with facilities management?

→ What about the roles of real estate professionals in relation to facilities management?

→ What are the relationships of environmental quality and facilities management?

→ What is the relationship of information systems to facilities management?

→ What is the relationship of records management to facilities management?

→ How can renovations best be managed as part of quality facilities management?

→ What are the roles of facilities management in the war on terrorism?

→ What are the fundamentals of security management as part of facilities management?

→ How can leaders best manage and motivate facilities management and other personnel?

So many people are asking and routinely considering these questions, and they want answers they understand and common-sense practical strategies they can use.

## *Scope*

This book is not designed to be a comprehensive descriptive textbook or reference that extensively covers the entire field of facilities management. There are many other good books that address various aspects of facilities management and address other possible approaches. This book contains Dr. Mark Langemo's views and my views of what works and what is less likely to work in the real world. It is based on our collective experience in facilities management, business management, information systems and records management, in consulting, extensive seminar work, and our over 75 years of combined business and professional experiences. It is our intent to provide very practical advice.

I recommend *High-Performance Facilities Management* for individuals new to facilities management, for those just starting a facilities management program, and for professional facilities managers who are always seeking to expand their knowledge as part of strengthening existing programs. Dr. Langemo and I wrote this book for facilities managers, facilities management staff members, and for leaders in the disciplines closely associated with facilities management. We wrote it for business executives and government administrators who are either directly or indirectly responsible for facilities management functions.

Mark Langemo and I also decided to write this book using the same words and style that we use in the executive briefings, management seminars, training seminars, and consulting sessions that we are each privileged to conduct. We believe that people need straightforward strategies, action plans, and step-by-step lists of what to do and how to do it to achieve high-performance facilities management. We include numerous additional sources of information, but it is not our intention to list every option or every reference. We do not want our readers to have to search all over for the answers but instead, we want potential and good answers to be clearly presented for our readers' thoughtful consideration.

One last comment. Every time we write together, conduct seminars together, work together, and when each of us is working independently, we try to motivate people. We try to excite people about the topics of facilities management and about our areas of professional expertise. We want to enable people to make multiple positive differences for other people and organizations through their work. We talk enthusiastically, and now you will see that we also write enthusiastically. We want our readers to read the same words that are heard by our students, seminar attendees, participants in executive briefings, attendees in training sessions, and participants in consulting meetings. So, for those who want the straight, unabridged version of our perspectives on facilities management, Mark Langemo and I offer you *High-Performance Facilities Management*.

Some special words of appreciation are in order.  I would like to thank my wonderful wife Jacque for her continuing love, support, encouragement, and confidence in me.  I know Mark expresses the same appreciation, admiration, and thanks to his wife, Diane, and to sons Steve, Brent, and Darrin.  Next, we would like to thank both Jean Clayton and Glen Clayton of Century Creations Printing/Knight Printing for their professional editing, formatting, publishing, and printing of this book.  And, we are so appreciative of all of our professional associates and friends who have told us "write that book and make it available to us just as soon as possible!"  You have individually and collectively motivated us to make *High-Performance Facilities Management* a reality.

*Daniel A. Brathal*

# Chapter 1
## *INTRODUCTION TO TOTAL WORKPLACE DESIGN AND MANAGEMENT*

Throughout history, humans have used their innate curiosity, creativity, ingenuity, imagination, and their vocational skills to create shelter, tools, machinery, equipment, processes, and systems that make living an easier, safer, healthier, and more enjoyable endeavor. Humans have used these same characteristics to generate goods and services for trade or for sale. A thriving, competitive, hectic, exciting, and dynamic world of commerce evolved and is the environment within which a majority of people now live and work.

Over a period of many centuries, hunters, gatherers, growers, builders, and people in a wide variety of trades working alone or in small groups gradually evolved an industrial society that concentrated primarily on manufacturing and the distribution of what was manufactured. Continuing evolution led to today's information society in which success, competitiveness, and quality of life depends heavily on technologically-augmented human endeavor. Over the years, all human beings involved in this evolution have needed spaces, places, tools, technology, and information in order to survive and thrive. And, they have needed these things in the right places, at the right times, in the right orders, in the right quantities, and at the right prices.

Shelter and some kind of space were essential in which to perform whatever activities were necessary for existence by individuals, families, and larger groups of people. Fundamental to any kind of commerce was the need for appropriate spaces and places to do their work.

Continued evolution of the human species required increasingly more sophisticated people, facilities, tools, technologies, and information systems in order to survive, be competitive, and to thrive. Inevitably, competition derived from commerce forced producers to make things bigger, faster, better, and cheaper. These factors accelerated demands for better spaces, places, tools, processes, and systems. Carefully crafted and provided spaces, increasingly larger and more complex facilities, steadily evolving information technology systems, and expanding needs of workers using

1

those resources have led to sophisticated management disciplines, techniques, facilities, technologies, and approaches for work accomplishment.

High-technology manufacturing facilities, sophisticated information systems, robotics and other computer-augmented systems, and related state-of-the-art resources have been developed and continue to emerge. They are all being utilized individually and in combination to make humans more productive, to improve qualities of goods and services, and to speed time-to-market. This is all done for purposes of becoming and remaining competitive in time-critical marketplaces and in a dynamic world economy and political environment. All of these objectives and needs have combined to result in huge requirements for appropriate spaces, places, and processes, and to have huge impacts on the planning, design, layout, construction, installation, and utilization of those spaces and places.

Ultimately, more and more people came to be involved in finding and providing appropriate spaces, creating good tools, constructing needed structures, and combining their efforts to maintain that which was built. Needs accelerated for what has evolved to be today's facilities management profession. Increasingly, more and more veteran facilities management professionals and colleague professionals in closely-related management disciplines—including the authors of this book—have come to believe that what is desirable and beneficial for the future are facilities management approaches that result in "total workplace design and management."

## *Who Wrote This Book?*

Dan Brathal spent nearly 33 years as an administrative executive for 3M Company headquartered in St. Paul, Minnesota—with 15 of the last 18 of those years as Manager, Corporate Site Management or Manager, Facilities Management Services. Dr. Mark Langemo, CRM, has spent 30 years as a senior university business professor and in consulting, management seminar, authorship, and related work. Most of his endeavors have been continually related to workplace development and management. Together, Dan and Mark have "been there and done that" and have collectively experienced almost all good, some bad, and the occasional ugly that goes with creating, equipping, and managing workplaces. Professional colleagues and good friends for over 30 years, this book is the third book that has resulted from Dan's and Mark's combined and continuing efforts to improve and enhance the work lives and personal lives of others.

2

The authors have increasingly come to believe that total workplace design and management is readily and practically achievable. They are convinced that total workplace design, development, and management fundamentals can be learned and implemented by individuals seeking to become well-rounded facilities management professionals or by veteran facilities management professionals seeking to fine tune and augment their knowledge and capabilities. Paramount in the authors' thinking is their deep beliefs about many realities of the places where people work, including:

→ People are the most valuable resource.

→ People need productive and effective places to work.

→ Work lives and personal lives are enhanced by high-quality workplaces.

→ Effective workplaces have multiple and significant impacts on personnel productivity and performance.

→ People want workplaces they appreciate, know to be adequate, and of which they can be proud.

→ Emotional, intellectual, physiological, and social needs must be fulfilled and enhanced through high-quality workplace development and management.

→ High-quality workplaces attract and retain high-quality professionals.

→ High-performance facilities management should be viewed as total workplace development and management.

→ Total workplace design and management contributes to total quality of life.

→ Successful facilities management is not a one-time effort but must be a continually evolving process.

→ High-performance workplaces are combinations of well-designed spaces, comfortable surroundings, appropriate technologies, and efficient environments for high-quality human interactions.

→ Totally-integrated workplaces require appropriate combinations of people, place, process, technology, and information.

- Architectural, behavioral, environmental, information and records management systems, medical, quality assurance, security, sociological and other components combine to be essential for total workplace design and management.

- Information is knowledge, and high-performance facilities management should enable efficient acquisition, creation, processing, distribution, use, and management of information.

- Facilities do not manage themselves—they require leaders who provide professional, creative, diligent, and consistent management.

- Facilities management is a profession that grows in importance and stature every day.

- Professional facilities management is a discipline that parallels other established management disciplines.

- Facilities management knowledge is not inherited but must be acquired, learned, and nurtured over time.

- Success as facilities management professionals requires learning a fundamental base of knowledge that must be kept up to date by continuing education.

- Total workplace development and management recognizes that all organizations are composed of parts—each of which must function well independently if organizations are to function well as entire entities.

- Success as facility management professionals requires integrating the knowledge, expertise, and experience of many colleagues in associated disciplines.

- Successful facilities management requires functioning in partnership with organizations' senior management.

- Facilities management professionals should not work in isolation and should be part of total management teams.

- What people help you plan, they will help you implement, use, manage, and preserve.

- What people help you plan, they will also help you present to others and encourage them to support.

- High-performance management of facilities contributes significantly and positively to organizations' profitability and the financial bottom line.

- Total workplace management significantly improves images and how organizations will be seen by others.

- High-quality workplaces contribute to legal and regulatory compliance.

- Competitive advantages expand exponentially when professional people use superior workplaces to achieve profitability and success.

- Total workplace management assumes commitments to caring about and protecting the resources of "God's green earth."

## *What is the IFMA?*

The International Facility Management Association (IFMA) was founded in 1980 and is an international professional association dedicated to its approximately 17,500 members within over 125 chapters spanning over 50 countries. IFMA sponsors and conducts research, provides educational progams, spots and monitors trends, and assists organizational and corporate facilities managers in developing strategies to manage facility, human, and real estate assets. The organization continues to grow along with an increasing awareness and understanding of the scope and contributions of this highly-specialized and now essential management discipline. Readers can access the IFMA website (www.ifma.com) to learn about the association, its goals and objectives, members, chapters, and related resources.

Professional people do the right things professionally, and the authors strongly and enthusiastically recommend that readers of this book join the IFMA and utilize the vast resources that can be accessed through the association. The potential for aggressive networking that includes finding, making contact with, meeting, and interacting with colleague facilities managers can be significant in terms of benefits that can be realized. Join and use the resources of IFMA.

## What is Facilities Management?

The definition "facility management is a profession that encompasses multiple disciplines to ensure functionality of the built environment by integrating people, place, process, and technology" is provided for the profession by IFMA on the association's website at (www.ifma.com). Further, the IFMA website presents that the 2000-2001 edition of the United States Bureau of Labor Statistics' Occupational Outlook Handbook includes a description of facility manager as an occupational category.

The following description (verbatim) offers an expanded view of this broad-based professional area. "Facility managers are assigned a wide range of tasks in planning, designing and managing facilities. They are responsible for coordinating the physical workplace with the people and work of an organization."

## What is the Work of Facilities Managers?

Performing these functions requires integrating the principles of business administration, architecture, and the behavioral and engineering sciences. Although the specific tasks assigned to facilities managers vary substantially depending on the organization, the duties typically fall into several categories. They include communications, environmental factors, facility function, finance, human factors, operations and maintenance, project planning and management, real estate, interior design, and quality assessment.

Responsibilities of facilities managers within these broad categories may include architectural planning and design, budgeting, lease management, purchase and sale of real estate, renovations, and space and workplace planning. Facilities managers may suggest and oversee renovation projects for a variety of reasons ranging from improving efficiency to ensuring that facilities meet government regulations and environmental, health, safety, and security standards. Additionally, facilities managers are responsible for continually monitoring facilities to ensure that they remain affordable, safe, secure, well maintained, and effective. Facilities managers are usually responsible for managing, motivating, and leading staff including administrative, engineering, maintenance, grounds, and custodial personnel.

## *Scope of Facilities Managers' Work and Impact*

The components of today's and tomorrow's total workplace design and management have combined to truly make the world smaller. It is now common for many of today's corporations and other organizations to have facilities and operations in many countries, states or provinces, and cities throughout the world. The wisdom of methodically applying and managing current architectural, design, construction, and facilities operations principles in any location around the world continues to be increasingly recognized as critical for achieving and maintaining competitive advantage and success.

The cost of labor, land, raw materials, transportation, and other infrastructure services is often lower in most countries outside of Canada and the United States of America. The point is that it requires very careful and comprehensive facilities and process planning in order to network and connect geographically dispersed facilities. This requirement also emphasizes the reality that many disciplines such as architecture, construction, environmental, facilities management, food, health, information management, information technology, mail, records management, telecommunications, and others are or should be involved with the effective design and development of totally capable facilities and totally successful companies or other organizations.

## *Become a Certified Facility Manager (CFM)*

The Certified Facility Manager (CFM) credential, within the profession of facilities management, is a respected global credential that sets the standard for ensuring the knowledge and abilities of practicing facilities managers. IFMA's certification process is designed to assess competency in the profession through work experience, education and the ability to pass a comprehensive examination. Since the program began in 1992, more than 3,500 facilities managers from over 25 countries have achieved this prestigious recognition.

Goals of the CFM exam process are to assure professional excellence in facilities management, to establish standards for professional practice, promote added value to the profession, and to influence future direction of the profession. For practicing facilities managers, becoming a Certified Facility Manager (CFM) distinguishes them in today's competitive job market, invests in their futures, demonstrates their leadership and initiative,

7

and contributes to the advancement of the profession. For information about the Certified Facility Manager (CFM) certification process, go to the IFMA website at www.ifma.com.

## *The Stakeholders of Facilities Management*

A list of the stakeholders (disciplines and internal or external functions or organizations) that should partner in total workplace design and management include:

➡ Architecture

➡ Audio and Visual Services

➡ Business Continuity Planning

➡ Civil Engineering

➡ Community Agencies (Police, Fire, Etc.)

➡ Construction

➡ Custodial Services

➡ Electrical Engineering

➡ Environmental Engineering

➡ Facilities Management

➡ Finance

➡ Food Services

➡ Grounds Maintenance

➡ Information Technology

➡ Interior Design

➡ Mail Services

➡ Maintenance

➡ Mechanical Engineering

➡ Medical/Industrial Hygiene and Toxicology

➡ Procurement

- Public Affairs

- Receptionists

- Records Management

- Safety Engineering

- Senior Management

- Security

- Shipping and Receiving

- Suppliers

- Telecommunications

- Tenants

- Transportation

- Utilities

The above is not an all-inclusive list and intentionally lists the stakeholders alphabetically rather than in order of importance. The level of importance and participation of each individual stakeholder often changes from project to project. But the list does illustrate that many stakeholders are typically involved with the planning, design, construction, development, provision, and operation of effective and efficient facilities.

The contributions of these diverse stakeholders of total workplace design and management will be many and varied. If all of these colleague disciplines do their jobs well every time, then the tenants occupying facilities should be able to do their work without having to invest their time in endeavors that other professionals can provide at lower costs and with greater quality. High-performance workplaces enable tenants to do their work without being distracted by the shortcomings of poor workplace design, operation, or management.

## Insights into the Evolution of Today's Total Workplace Design and Management

A virtual revolution in workplace environments took place during the decades of the 1970s and 1980s. Owners, corporate executives, government administrators, and leaders in many organizations became increasingly more aware of the potential to leverage human capacities and skills through the development of improved facilities, equipment, technologies, processes, and through increased emphases on quality.

Foreign competition was steadily increasing, customers were demanding higher quality products and services, and there were steadily increasing labor costs. Increased worker awareness about meeting the needs of disabled individuals, excitement about the potential of ergonomics, more awareness of the need for clean indoor air, and related issues resulted in growing demands for effective and efficient workplaces.

These interests spawned hundreds and perhaps thousands of new businesses that started providing and that continue to provide products and services to address the increasing demand for high-performance workplaces that are managed well. Demand increased for flexible furniture systems with better ergonomic features and for better quality of indoor air. Workers also demanded better communication systems, better and more powerful information technologies and systems, and more healthy and safe working environments. Personnel at all levels increasingly realized that substantially improved facilities led to overall improvements of work life. All of these elements combined to emphasize the potential of total workplace design and management.

## *New Prestige for Facilities Management*

The acceleration of awareness about and higher demands for more appropriate facilities elevated facilities management to higher levels of importance in the eyes and thinking of senior management, executives, and workers at all levels. Senior leaders and personnel at all levels increasingly wanted to be assured that their workplaces were safe and healthy and at the same time were protecting both indoor and outdoor environments as well as protecting the company or organization. The awareness and concern for both indoor and outdoor environmental factors was also receiving more public attention and more management and personnel concern.

Results included the decade of the 1990s being very good for facilities management programs and facilities management professionals. Prior to and including the 1990s, there was the development and introduction of several new laws and regulations related to clean indoor air, emission controls, OSHA, EPA, accessibility, and many other safety, health, and environmental issues. These laws and regulations and those that have followed have had and continue to have huge ripple effects throughout the facilities management industry and profession. Decade 2000 will continue to see steady elevations of facilities management as a function essential to the success, competitiveness, and financial bottom line of organizations.

## Positive Responses from Suppliers and Colleague Professionals

Furniture manufacturers generally became very sensitive to ergonomic and flexibility demands from customers. Carpet manufacturers have become increasingly sensitive to product quality, visual appeal, acoustics, air quality, and other environmental issues. It is obvious that manufacturers and other providers of services had vested interests in terms of selling more products and gaining more customers. However, much to their credit, they—individually and collectively—increased their research, development, and commitment to providing components that would contribute to total, safe, healthy, and productive workplace design and management.

Security and safety managers have become even more concerned about worker protection, safety, and overall well being. Environmental specialists are individually and collectively managing an ever-increasing array of regulatory guidelines that require daily diligence in order to assure that all environmental protection and reporting is done in compliance with legal requirements. These and comparable contributions from colleague specialists continue to move forward the development of total workplace design and management.

## Facilities Management Challenges in the Immediate Future

Today and in the years immediately to come, organizations in both the private and public sectors will increasingly be striving to cope with expansion, contraction, consolidation, dispersion, rightsizing, and intensifying competitive business factors. Facilities managers and colleague managers in our information society environments will be striving to deal with growth or decreases in sales and workforces fluctuating in numbers. Running lean and with fewer resources available proportionate to those of years gone by will likely be common.

Successfully confronting issues that arise out of broadly distributed workforces will require astute leadership. How to foster effective communication at a time of e-mail, e-records, and e-almost everything will continue to be challenges. Home officing, telecommuting, and emerging systems needing to be managed in global operating environments will be real and significant challenges to facilities managers and to colleague managers in stakeholder and related disciplines. Facilities managers today need to know more than their counterparts of only a few years ago. And, facilities management professionals of the future will need to be multi-disciplinary professionals to a greater extent than many of them may have believed at the time they entered the facilities management profession.

## *Excitement about the Future*

The potential for facilities managers individually and collectively, and for the facilities management profession, may never have been brighter. Appreciation by astute senior management and other senior leaders for high-performance facilities management programs, functions, systems, and for facilities managers may well be at an all-time high. The future can and will be bright for those facilities management professionals who accept the challenges of keeping their knowledge and skills as current-to-the-moment as reasonably possible.

The exchange of ideas is a powerful element in today's collaborative workplace. It is critically important that businesses and organizations of all types and sizes be able to maximize the intelligence, knowledge, education, experiences, observations, skills, talents, and values of increasingly diverse workforces. It is and will continue to be the job of every leader and manager to understand the culture of workplaces and to recognize and capitalize on the synergies that can emerge from those diverse workforces.

It will be a responsibility of facilities managers and other colleague operations managers to combine their knowledge, expertise, and experience to first articulate the need for high-quality workplaces and then to translate those needs into total workplace design and management. High-Performance Facilities Management has been written for facilities management professionals and other readers seeking to achieve those objectives.

12

## Summary

A thriving, competitive, exciting, and dynamic world of commerce is the environment within which a majority of people now live and work. Continued evolution increasingly required more sophisticated facilities, tools, technologies, and information systems in order to survive, be competitive, and to thrive. The authors of this book along with many other veteran facilities management professionals have come to believe that what is essential, desirable, and beneficial for the future are facilities management approaches that result in "totally integrated workplace design and management."

Co-authors Dan Brathal and Mark Langemo have over 75 years of combined facilities management and business experience. They have increasingly come to believe that totally integrated workplace design and management is readily and practically achievable. The co-authors have deep beliefs about what is highly desirable about places where people work. And, they are convinced that total workplace design, development, and management can be learned and implemented by individuals seeking to become well-rounded facilities management professionals.

What is facilities management, the IFMA, the work of facilities managers, the scope of facilities managers' work and impact, and how to become a Certified Facility Manager (CFM) are discussed in this chapter. Special emphasis is given to identifying the stakeholders (disciplines and internal or external functions or organizations) that should partner in total workplace design and management. The co-authors believe there will be exciting new prestige and multiple opportunities for facilities managers and stakeholders who seek to achieve high-performance facilities management.

# Chapter 2
## *CRITICAL IMPORTANCE OF INTEGRATED WORKPLACE DESIGN AND MANAGEMENT*

### *"The Whole Is Greater Than the Sum of Its Parts"*

Places where people live or work do not manage themselves. They require commitments and attention by individuals who have vested interests in seeing that they are cared for and maintained. If places where people live or work are ignored, they can quickly deteriorate into settings that people do not appreciate, respect, use appropriately, or continue to maintain as well as necessary. Further deterioration then tends to occur, and soon the living spaces or workplaces may be relegated to the status of old places in which few take pride or want to inhabit and use.

We must be concerned with total spaces, either total living spaces or total workplaces. Homes today are not typically just a room where an individual or a family prepares and eats food, another room where individuals sleep, and another room used for washing and grooming. Homes commonly are all the places where individuals and families live—entrances, living rooms, great rooms, kitchens, bedrooms, home offices, bathrooms, garages, lawns and other surrounding spaces, and the decorative treatments applied to make all of those spaces pleasant.

Workplaces today and in the future are not and will not be just one individual's office, workstation, or desk in an office building. Workplaces combine to be all the places in which individuals work. Total workplaces—for example—may include offices, workstations, desks, reception areas, conference rooms, break rooms, training rooms, computer centers, records rooms, corridors or hallways, cafeterias, fitness centers, parking garages, and the decorative treatments used to enhance the appearance and enjoyment of those spaces.

Thinking, collaborating, creating information, receiving information, processing information, making decisions, managing, motivating, and leading are continuous major functions performed within today's workplaces. Because a majority of employed persons now work in or from an office base, the development of appropriate workplaces is fundamental to the success of organizations. Actually, in today's information society populated predominately by knowledge workers, workplaces can be viewed as extending to include homes, home offices, hotels, restaurants, airports and airline clubs, lounges, airplanes, and automobiles. Any place where people can think, read, write, and communicate can be viewed as extended workplaces.

## The Workplace Situation in Many Organizations Today

What is the current workplace situation in organizations and offices where you are a stakeholder of some kind? The following descriptions apply to an amazing number of organizations that are small, medium, or huge in size—and in private, government, or not-for-profit organizations.

Everyone recognizes and agrees that places to work are necessary and that they should be planned, used, and managed well. Most agree that the information explosion continues and that volumes of e-mail, electronic records, paper documents, and other records created and used by people are steadily increasing. No one disputes that computers, computer peripherals, software, phones, and related technologies continue to evolve and change quickly in their forms, size, modes of use, and places of use. And, almost everyone admits that while they may have strong likes and dislikes about their workplaces, they really are not sure about how workplaces can best be developed and managed in today's organizations.

A major problem in many organizations is the existence of an organizational mindset that just superficially suggests "this is our building and these are our spaces for individuals." Individuals then employed are usually just assigned an amount of space, often based on a combination of looking at what space is available and on what space is currently assigned to co-workers. Sometimes, only minimal attention is given to how the individual inhabitants will need to interact and communicate with others or what technologies they will need to do the work expected of them. Many people are simply expected to adjust to their surroundings, make do as well as they can, and essentially scrounge for what they need but often do not have available to them.

An associated problem continues to be extensive decentralized control of spaces, workplaces, and facilities within organizations. For example, in many organizations, a given department or work group is often assigned

16

to one floor of a building—and then is expected to adjust as necessary to accommodate the personnel of that unit. In the same organization, another department or work group is assigned to another floor of the building—and is similarly expected to adjust as necessary to accommodate the personnel of that unit.

A subsequent walkthrough of both those departments or units may often result in seeing some employees in spacious work areas with many amenities available to them while finding other employees literally cramped into closet-size spaces. Managerially, leaders of units, departments, or workgroups within organizations deserve more than to be left more or less on their own to resolve issues about how their workplaces should be developed, used, and managed.

Decentralized control of spaces and places for work generally should be abandoned in favor of developing senior-management supported, centrally-managed, organization-wide facilities management programs. Leaders in North American business, industry, and government learned years ago that creating organization-wide and centrally-managed accounting, finance, IT, and human resources management programs resulted in much more stable on-going management of total organizations. Similarly, today's and tomorrow's organizations will benefit in multiple ways from the establishment of organization-wide centrally-managed facilities management programs under the direction of professional facilities managers.

Another problem in so many organizations is the fact that the formal educational level about the planning, design, construction, renovation, use, and management of places to work is quite low. Although most individuals evolve their own definitions of what they like and do not like in their workplaces, few have ever taken formal university courses or have ever participated in programs or seminars devoted specifically to the development of high-performance workplaces. As a result, many senior leaders do not understand or appreciate the scope of professional facilities management and they often are not sure how successful facilities management programs should and can be developed and managed. Unfortunately, many of them are also not accustomed to providing the leadership, management support, funding, and staffing needed for appropriate organization-wide facilities management programs.

Financial investments in spaces and places for work have often not been adequate, appropriate, or realistic given the real workplace needs of workers individually and collectively. Throughout the 1960s and 1970s, financial investments were often made just to make sure there was enough space for the organization but without methodically or scientifically completing an appropriate analysis of organizational needs. Many times, the coordinated planning necessary to result in the acquisition, renovation, or construction of integrated workplaces prepared for on-going professional facilities management was not done.

Today, that reluctance or failure to invest back then in comprehensive programs for organization-wide facilities management is now catching up with many organizations. The establishment of IFMA in 1980 was one of many initiatives that increasingly led to improvement of many facilities management situations. That development and other good work by facilities management professionals during those years led to a growing understanding today that what was and is really needed is totally integrated workplace design and management.

## Twenty Major Benefits of High-Performance Facilities Management Programs

Organizations will benefit in many ways and will realize multiple returns on their investments from the establishment of organization-wide centrally-managed facilities management programs. Twenty major benefits of high-performance facilities management programs include:

➡ *Increased Executive, Managerial, and Operational Effectiveness.* If leaders and professionals at all levels have workplaces developed and integrated appropriately to result in their having almost instant access to the technology, human interaction, and communications essential to them, they can perform their functions, do their work, and take care of people they need to serve. Coordination of facilities management throughout organizations can be achieved by centralizing control of facilities management functions instead of continuing many current decentralized situations in which people are struggling to manage and adjust to their workplaces as well as they can.

➡ *Measurable Increases in Worker Productivity.* If personnel at all levels have almost instant access to the technology, human interaction, communications, and information and records essential to them, then they can do their work and meet the needs of internal and external customers and all people to be served. If they do not have access to those resources, then work is usually delayed, people's needs are not met, and adverse consequences result.

➡ ***Leveraging the Expertise and Experience of Colleague Professionals.*** Totally integrated workplace design and management should include colleague professionals from closely related disciplines working closely together to capitalize on their combined expertise and experience. Architects, custodial services managers, engineers, environmental specialists, facilities managers, food service managers, health care specialists, and information technology leaders all have valuable knowledge to share. Essential input should also come from interior designers, maintenance managers, procurement managers, records managers, safety specialists, shipping and receiving managers, security specialists, and related professionals who all possess valuable knowledge that contributes to totally integrated workplace design and management.

➡ ***Legal Defensibility.*** In today's legal environment, organizations are vulnerable to adverse judgments if workers or other personnel are injured or harmed in virtually any way while spending time within workplaces. To be positioned well relative to potential legal defensibility, there needs to be professional facilities management programs developed with organization-wide policies and procedures developed and implemented to include environmental, health, safety, and security provisions for all people within intelligently integrated workplaces.

➡ ***Compliance with Federal, State, Local Government, and Industry-Specific Legal and Regulatory Requirements.*** There is a steadily increasing body of federal, state, and local government laws and regulations continually evolving through the efforts of the EPA, ADA, OSHA, and other relevant agencies as well as from legislative and governmental units that impact on facilities and their occupancy and use. Well-designed forward-looking facilities management programs should enable avoiding or minimizing costly fines or other penalties as well as reducing risks in civil litigation and government investigations. But more importantly, compliance with applicable laws and regulations contributes to the assurance of long-term welfare for personnel occupying facilities.

19

- **Improved Customer Service.**  Improved customer service is a major benefit of totally integrated workplace design and management.  Reality is that if needed information and records, needed technologies, needed human interactions, and needed communications can be almost instantly accessed, then people needing service can be served.  On the other hand, if customers or other people are expected to wait because of inadequate workplaces while searches take place for resources, some of those people seeking service will take their business someplace else.  Good facilities design, development, and management promote good service to the constituents, customers, clients, patients, students, and others served by organizations.

- **Maximized Value of Organizational Personnel.**  The most expensive and most important resource in any organization is the people who are employed by an organization.  Typically, almost $9 out of every $10 spent for administrative work accomplishment is spent to pay the salaries and benefits of organizational personnel.  Maximizing investments in expensive people is increasingly realized when their workplaces are designed around them and around productive ways of performing their work rather than expecting them to conform to constraints of inflexible facilities.

- **Maximized Value of Investments in Structures.**  Spaces within structures are expensive.  Whether workplaces are developed within buildings that are constructed new and are owned, within renovated older buildings which are owned, or are within leased facilities, these spaces are expensive.  It is always essential to the success of organizations to provide the spaces and workplaces necessary to house operations for accomplishment of work.  Additionally, it is essential that organizations, along with reasonable provisions for needed expansion, avoid paying for facilities that would be in excess of what is needed immediately.

- **Maximize Use of Standards.**  An almost universal human trait is that of wanting and expecting to be treated fairly.  Intelligent people know and understand that being treated fairly doesn't always mean being treated the same, but it does mean being treated fairly over time.  Organization-wide and centrally-managed facilities management programs should be implemented including and complete with the creation of well-researched and carefully crafted

facilities standards. Well-thought-out standards for space allocations, space locations, equipment and technology assignments,
and for amenities and conditioning of space will result in lower
costs and in higher personnel morale.

➡ ***Leveraging Financial Capital.*** Consolidation of purchases, enjoy-
ing the benefits of volume discounts, assuring compatibility of
component and technology systems, and maximizing the value of
construction spending all contribute to wise use of capital. Obtaining
multiple service or renovation contracts at lower costs, achieving
economies of scale, and optimizing financial alternatives open to
larger financial transactions are all ways that total workplace design
and management contributes to leveraging financial capital.

➡ ***Reduced Operating Costs.*** Reduced costs of operating facilities
can be achieved in several ways. Not paying for more facilities
than are needed, completing careful analyses to determine appropriate and not excessive levels of lighting and heating, maximizing utilization of shared available facilities, and through making
reduced operating costs high priorities can all result in reduced
costs. There is an insidious nature to operating costs. If not
carefully managed, they will subtly, discretely, and surely increase
at rates greater than organizations should need to endure.
Minimizing wasteful spending and increasing buying power through
totally integrated workplace design and management can result
in handsome financial rewards.

➡ ***Ease of Access by Police, Fire, OSHA, and Other Responders.***
Organizations of all sizes and types must be accessible by paramedics, health care providers, fire departments, law enforcement
agencies, OSHA representatives, regulatory bodies, and security
personnel—especially in the event of emergencies. Well-developed
procedures that accommodate emergency responders and other personnel should be components of totally integrated workplace environments.

➡ ***Coordinated Planning for Rapid Access to Information and
Records.*** Records are the memory of organizations and are the
essential raw material for making decisions, accomplishing work,
and serving people. If information (e-mail, electronic records,
paper documents, microfilm, or other records) is almost instantly
available when needed, then people needing service can be served.

21

➡️ **Coordinated Planning for Maximized Use of Technologies.** All organizations within business, industry, government, not-for-profit, professional, institutional, and other entities have increasing arrays of high-technology systems available for their use. Maximizing the uses and values of those technologies will always be highly dependent upon well coordinated planning for placement of, access to, safe use of, and security for those technology components and systems.

➡️ **Reduced Storage Requirements for Records.** Totally integrated workplace design and management assumes that facilities managers will be routinely collaborating with colleague managers in other disciplines, including records managers, relative to all aspects of space and workplace planning. Implementation of records management programs within organizations often results in the potential to reduce current paper records volumes and all records volumes by 30 to 40 percent. Additionally, analysis usually reveals that additional volumes of paper records are candidates for conversion to digital or microfilm form. Records managers and facilities managers working together can often substantially reduce storage spaces, storage equipment, lighting, and electricity required for management of records.

➡️ **Maximizing Availability of Amenities.** A human tendency is that of wanting goods, services, and conveniences—and wanting them now! Totally integrated workplace design and management should include making appropriate provisions for those amenities deemed to be most important by personnel of organizations. Such amenities may include cafeterias, food service vendors, day care programs, fitness centers, company stores, hair stylists and barber shops, dry cleaning services, shoe repair, ATMs, check cashing, motor vehicle licensing, entertainment event ticket sales, and other services.

➡️ **Elevation of the Images of Organizations.** It is not always the quality of meat that sells meat, often it is how that meat is packaged and what image or images about eating that meat may mean to potential consumers. How the public sees organizations and how much prestige will be associated with those images will always be affected either positively or negatively by organizations' facilities. Facilities management professionals are routinely mak-

ing contributions to maintaining high levels of organizational vis-
ibility, prestige, and success through totally integrated workplace
design and management.

➥ ***Capitalize on Creativity and Innovation.*** Co-author Mark
Langemo once thought he was going to make a living for a time
playing professional baseball, primarily as a catcher. He soon
learned that having a cannon for an arm didn't help him hit good
curveballs. By that time, back problems and pain routinely gave
him enough trouble so that constructing a desk which could
effortlessly be adjusted from a sit-down desk to a stand-up desk
was important to him for his work as a university professor, consultant, seminar leader, and author. Totally integrated workplace
design and management approaches foster capitalizing on creativity and innovation. If you need special facilities, equipment,
furnishings, or accessories to meet special needs, invent them, build
them, and provide them.

➥ ***Facilitate Business Continuity Planning.*** Risk management
initiatives in today's and tomorrow's organizations should include
well-developed and specific business continuity plans. Often referred
to as "disaster recovery planning," plans are essential for the continuation of operations and organizations in the event of terrorism, other human-created or natural disasters, or other adverse
events. Facilities managers need to be key leaders in the development of these plans because human evacuation, safety, and
protection are the most critical components of these plans. Facilities
managers, records managers, business continuity managers, and
IT managers should combine their efforts to make sure that all
vital information, vital records, and essential and vital systems
necessary for restoration and continuation of business are identified and appropriately backed up and protected. Business continuity planning is now among the very most important components in the work of professional facilities managers.

➥ ***High Personnel Morale.*** Totally integrated workplace design
and management typically results in employees feeling better
about themselves, feeling better about their work, and in their
placing higher values on their workplaces—all of which usually
results in higher levels of individual employee motivation. And,
it is the motivation of each individual within a group that com-

bines to make up a group's morale. Great personnel morale will always be an incredibly valuable asset for any organization while poor morale will work against any leader and any organization.

## Achieving Competitive Advantage and Impacting the Bottom Line

There are no valid reasons for being a not-for-profit organization unless you really truly genuinely want to be one. All corporations (excluding not-for-profit organizations) and virtually all business organizations want, need, and expect to make money. All government organizations at all levels are challenged with managing and stretching appropriated and earned dollars to enable providing maximum amounts of services for the funding available. Totally integrated facilities management programs and professional facilities managers can make major contributions to achieving competitive advantage and to positively impacting the financial bottom line.

When senior managers have access to facilities, information, technologies, and other resources they need in order to lead, they can make effective and efficient use of their time in leadership processes, and then corporations usually make money or government organizations usually save money. When personnel at all levels have the facilities, information, technologies, and resources readily available to do their work, then corporations usually make more money and government entities usually save more money. Each of the twenty major benefits of high-quality facilities management programs discussed in this chapter can contribute directly to achieving competitive advantage and positively impacting the financial bottom line. But the real power comes from achieving those benefits in combination and capitalizing on the power of human endeavor coupled with many or all of these benefits in order to save money and to make money.

Valuing people and enabling expensive people to have feelings of worth and of pride in their workplaces all leads to increased individual motivation, collective morale, increased productivity and efficiency. All of these outcomes from totally integrated workplace design and management combine to positively impact on saving money and on making money.

## The 3M Totally Integrated Workplace Experience

3M Company was founded as Minnesota Mining and Manufacturing Company in 1902 in Two Harbors, Minnesota. Initial products were abrasives and sandpaper technologies. The company was moved to Duluth, Minnesota, and in the early 1900s to St. Paul, Minnesota. The growth and prosperity of 3M genuinely deserves the accolade of being a great American corporate success story.

Today, 3M Company employs approximately 70,000 people in operations spanning more than 60 countries. Principal product groups include automotive, consumer, electronic, health care, industrial, office, safety, and many other continually emerging product lines. A research-oriented company renowned for its introduction of innovative new products, 3M had a long-standing corporate objective of generating at least 30 percent of annual revenue from products introduced within the past four years.

Impressive and exciting facts about 3M Company include its selection for several years as one of America's most well managed companies. And, 3M has also been selected for several years through national surveys as one of America's most desirable places to work.

Co-author Dan Brathal was Manager, Corporate Site Management; Manager, Office Planning; or Manager, Facilities Management during 15 of his last 18 years at 3M. He was in records management at 3M for 14 years, the last five as Corporate Records Manager, before being assigned to the facilities management leadership positions. Associates with long and distinguished careers whose work combined to build 3M's corporate Facilities Management Department were James R. "Jim" Jensen and William V. "Bill" Nygren. Dan strongly believes that 3M's many achievements in totally integrated workplace design and management are directly attributable to the long-term strategic thinking, planning, and on-going dynamic leadership of both Jim Jensen and Bill Nygren.

The practice of structured facilities management at 3M became a corporate entity in 1976 under the leadership of Jim Jensen and evolved to its present identity as the Corporate Facilities Management Department in 1986. Notable achievements through all the history of Corporate Facilities Management at 3M include:

➥ Creation in the mid 1980s of a senior-level Corporate Facilities Planning and Utilization Committee which formally acknowledged the need for senior corporate management to be intimately involved in establishing facilities development and operations strategies. This committee included vice presidents of administration, engineering, finance, human resources, manufacturing, and office administration in addition to line division representatives.

➥ Substantially enabled increases in worker productivity through managing facility growth rates of only about 2 percent during many years when 3M was growing sales at rates averaging 10 percent annually. These ratios were achieved through a combination of improved office layout and design, installation of improved workstation components, improved deployment of technology, managed records retention and disposition, and on-going analyses of how to best support employee productivity through totally integrated workplace design and management.

➥ Facilities Management sponsored establishment and operation of safety, health, and environment teams within 3M facilities which included first-response capabilities to medical emergencies, fires, hazardous materials handling, and for substance spills. These teams conducted environmental audits along with safety audits and facilitated correction of risky situations.

➥ The Corporate Facilities Manager was selected as a member of a Health, Safety, Environment, and Transportation Committee along with directors of plant engineering, corporate safety, and Chair of the corporation's Technical Council. Safe lab practices, safe hazardous materials handling, adherence to environmental regulations, compliance with OSHA regulations, and general application of health, safety, and environmental best practices were responsibilities of this Committee. The group routinely drew on the expertise and experience of colleague professionals in specialty fields throughout the company for purposes of achieving totally integrated, safe, and healthy workplace design and management.

➥ While having a long and admired history of operating in compliance with regulatory requirements, 3M's legal defensibility was even more enhanced through consistent and careful attention to workplace conditions and strict adherence to regulatory requirements with the outcome that lawsuits resulting from workplace injury or harm were negligible. 3M's analysis and documentation of workplace conditions and regulatory compliance was consistently respected by OSHA, EPA, and other inspectors.

➡ Many contributions to high-quality customer service were attributable in part to employees with high levels of motivation and morale. They were also generally happy in their work environments and equipped appropriately to do their work. Happy personnel are usually productive personnel, and their genuine enthusiasm routinely rubbed off on customers and others with whom they interacted.

➡ Facilities Management at 3M had landlord responsibilities for 50+ buildings of significant size on the St. Paul campus of 3M and closely surrounding areas. Preventive maintenance programs were in place in all of those buildings. Construction and equipment specifications were always on the high side of specifications as part of continuing 3M's commitment to high quality. Buildings were well planned, well constructed, and well maintained.

➡ Company-wide standards that were developed and implemented for totally integrated workplace design and management included those for workstations and furniture. Standards were in place for indoor air quality, light levels, power supplies, laboratory procedural practices, hazardous materials packaging and transportation, telecommunications systems, and for operations of heating, ventilation, and air conditioning systems.

➡ Excellent contracts were negotiated for purchase of furnishings, equipment, carpeting, and technologies through 3M's procurement processes. As a result, 3M received maximum quantities and qualities of products and services because of carefully planned and coordinated purchasing and the ability to leverage capital through transactions of substantial sizes.

➡ Reduced operating costs were achieved on a consistent basis by routinely renegotiating lease contracts and taking advantage of space available for lease in properties within close geographic proximity to other 3M facilities. Operating costs were also reduced regularly and consistently through construction of high-quality buildings, maintaining them well, and assuring that all infrastructure components were operating at appropriate levels. A major effort initiated in the early 1990s resulted in formal energy reduction programs that continue to achieve energy cost savings to this day.

- Feedback from responder services such as medical care providers, fire departments, law enforcement agencies, OSHA and other inspectors routinely indicated that 3M's record of accessibility and cooperation was excellent.

- 3M's Corporate Records Management Department and 3M's Corporate Facilities Management Department worked in a close partnership. Together they accomplished, in addition to other achievements, the development and implementation of standards and specifications for filing equipment, accessories, and supplies. Consequently, the 3M Corporate Records Management Department was the winner of an international prestigious Olsten Award for Excellence in Records Management.

- 3M Facilities Management on a formal and scheduled basis partnered with IT in the development of facilities that support telecommunications infrastructure. The development of forecasts and budgets for telecommunications infrastructure systems (fiber optic cables, wire cables, and related components) were implemented.

- Reductions in paper records volumes were and continue to be achieved through a combination of records retention schedule implementation, conversions of some records to microfilm or digital formats, through development of appropriate decentralized records rooms, and operation of a corporate records retention facility. Facilities Management Department and Records Management Department leaders worked closely together to achieve these objectives. That partnership also resulted in virtually no additional filing cabinets being purchased for the 50+ buildings at 3M Center for almost fifteen years.

- 3M Center in St. Paul, Minnesota, included over 50 major buildings on a 425-acre campus and immediately surrounding areas. With thousands of personnel commuting to 3M every day and with there being some distances to many stores and services needed by company personnel, a commitment was made to provide many of those amenities at 3M Center. Amenities readily available to employees included three company stores, sundry shops, two barbershops, multiple ATMs, a banking operation, dry cleaning drop-off and pickup, shoe repair drop-off and pickup, and other services.

- Visitors to 3M facilities worldwide were consistent in reporting high levels of appreciation, amazement, and respect for the design, construction, maintenance, operation, and over-all elegance of the company's buildings and grounds. Company personnel continue to be collectively proud of the company's distinction as one of America's best companies for which to work. 3M's image of being a somewhat conservative but forward-thinking technologically advanced successful company continues to be reflected in building architecture and facilities.

- 3M's Facilities Management Department routinely partnered with internal product divisions in the development, testing, and application of 3M products. Examples include fire-retardant sealers, construction adhesives, commercial cleaning products and equipment, ergonomic accessories for workstations, air filtration products, and security systems among many others.

- Business continuity planning was a high priority within 3M through ongoing cooperation between the Facilities Management Department, Business Continuity Services, IT, Records Management, Security, Safety, Environmental Services, manufacturing, and research organizations. One of the achievements of that work was the identification, assessment, and selection of a standard software package made available to document all corporate business continuity plans.

- 3M facilities consistently score high in employee opinion surveys with employees reporting high favorability and appreciation for the quality of the places in which they work. Historically, 3M has been known for the high caliber of its people, for long-term retention of personnel, and for consistently excellent workforce morale.

## Summary

Totally integrated workplace design and management is now more critical than ever to the success of organizations. Important for facilities managers and other leaders to know is the fact that if integrated workplace design and management is made an organizational objective, it is very likely that many benefits will be realized and that the facilities whole will be greater than the sum of its individual parts. Twenty major benefits and potential returns on investment of totally integrated workplace design and management were discussed in this chapter. Finally, major facilities management achievements in one of America's most well managed companies were highlighted.

# Chapter 3
## ENGAGING SENIOR MANAGEMENT
## IN FACILITIES MANAGEMENT ENDEAVORS

***If Senior Management Decides to Make Something a High Priority It Gets Approved, Funded, Staffed, and Accomplished! If Senior Management Doesn't Seem to Care, Progress Will be Difficult!***

A review of successful organization-wide facilities management programs usually reveals that those programs have been formally established by authorizing boards (Board of Directors, the Senior Partners, the City Council, Board of County Commissioners, or comparable board) as ongoing programs within organizations. Establishment of programs should be accomplished, ideally, following the development of strategic plans for facilities management. Strategic plans for facilities management need to be carefully developed and correlated with overall strategic plans, goals, and objectives of entire organizations.

Formal facilities management programs established by authorizing boards and/or senior management means that those programs will be established as continuing programs, not just facilities management projects or other short-term processes. Formally established facilities management programs typically are included as line items in budgets and have funding provided for continued program staffing even if personnel changes take place. Strong authorizing board support and strong senior management support is absolutely essential for facilities management programs to operate successfully.

Reality is that if owners, boards of directors, and senior executives strongly support facilities management programs, then programs can be developed, implemented, maintained over time, be very successful, and also generate many benefits and positive returns. On the other hand, if an authorizing board and senior executives do not really seem to care whether or not there is a facilities management program, then there is little likelihood that a program can be developed and operated successfully over a long period of time.

31

The individuals selected to be facilities managers will always be of major importance to the development of successful programs. Just as selecting the right person to be a Director of Information Systems, Director of Accounting and Finance, Director of Human Resources, or Director of Marketing is critical to the success of those functions, it is extremely important that an appropriate individual is named to the position of Facilities Manager.

Qualifications for the position of Facilities Manager should include an appropriate academic background, demonstrated work experience with facilities management responsibilities, and obvious aspirations to be a professional facilities manager. Many organizations now recruit only Certified Facility Managers (CFMs) for the position—or state "CFM preferred" to convey clearly that candidates must aspire to earn the CFM designation.

## *Organizational Location of Facilities Management Functions*

It is important to place the facilities management function as high as possible in organizational structures if maximum impact is to be made by facilities management programs, systems, policies, and procedures. If facilities management programs are buried down several levels in organizations, there are often inherent difficulties in program implementation and in achieving full benefits.

Organizational placement of facilities management programs varies. Successful programs exist as stand-alone units and as parts of or reporting to administrative services organizations, accounting and finance units, or other organizational entities. Precedents within respective industries (similar types of organizations) are often key factors in determining organizational location of facilities management programs and functions.

## *A Facilities Manager Can Not Do It Alone*

No one individual can single-handedly manage all aspects of totally integrated workplace design and management for organizations, especially in larger organizations. Therefore, additional facilities management expertise and personnel will usually be required.

As facilities management programs are established and facilities managers selected, next should come the careful determination and selection of specialists to make up appropriate facilities management organizations.

Depending on the size and complexity of organizations, those specialists may include architects, engineers, facilities designers, custodial supervisors, maintenance supervisors, and related personnel.

## *Create a Facilities Planning and Utilization Committee*

Similar to the 3M example mentioned in Chapter 2, a Facilities Planning and Utilization Committee (or comparable title) should be established and scheduled to meet periodically for purposes of providing support, in many meaningful ways, for facilities management programs. Members of Facilities Planning and Utilization Committees should usually include several representatives of organizations' senior management. Vice presidents of administration, engineering, finance, human resources, and manufacturing (or comparable positions), should be included as well as management representatives of each division, agency, department, or unit that makes up the organization. These committees should function at high levels within organizational structures.

Tremendous value derives from the cross section of business perspectives provided by leaders and representatives of different divisions, departments, branches, and workgroups that make up any organization and are included on an organization's Facilities Planning and Utilization Committee. While all these members are challenged to meet their own individual and workgroup business objectives, they must realize that putting aside personal or workgroup territorial interests and compromising are occasionally essential for meeting organization-wide needs and objectives.

Agendas for meetings of Facilities Planning and Utilization Committees should include assessments of current facilities management situations, collective identification of facilities management needs of organizations, prioritization of those needs, and discussions related to all aspects of totally integrated workplace development and management. Facilities management strategic plans, organization-wide policies and procedure reviews, and related facilities issues can all be enhanced through creative use of these committees.

When a Facilities Planning and Utilization Committee places its seal of approval on an initiative or project, other members of senior management typically add their approval and support. Whether it is site selection; construction projects; facility acquisitions; renovation projects; major lease negotiations; maintenance programs; security programs; business continuity plans; programs for protection against terrorism; health, safety, and environmental programs; or other issues, support of the Committee is very powerful. Presenting and securing support for all of these initiatives is ultimately much easier and credibility is significantly enhanced for the Facilities Manager and all Facilities Management Department personnel when the weight and support of that substantial committee exists.

## *More About Engaging Senior Management Support*

Facilities managers cannot develop organization-wide facilities management programs in a vacuum. The old adage that "what people understand, believe in, and help you plan, they will also support and help you carry out" applies directly to the potential success of organization-wide totally integrated workplace design and management.

Business owners, senior corporate executives, senior government administrators, and leaders in all organizations know and understand, of course, that spaces and places for people to work will be essential. But what they might not know or have experienced to any extent in their own backgrounds is how workplaces can most appropriately be acquired, planned and constructed, or otherwise made available and then be managed effectively.

Senior leaders typically have "big picture" aspirations, visions, dreams, missions, goals, objectives, and generalized plans for what they hope organizations should eventually be. Major roles of senior leaders include conceptualizing, setting, and articulating overall directions for organizations. Microsoft Corporation is the organization it is today in large part because a highly-intelligent, perceptive, forward-thinking leader—Bill Gates—envisioned and then dynamically led its creation and development. A recent visit to Microsoft's headquarters in Redmond, Washington, by one of this book's co-authors for purposes of consulting and conducting training seminars, confirmed that the fantastic multi-building campus of Microsoft has steadily evolved and brings reality to Mr. Gates' visions and strategic plans.

Senior leaders in all organizations are responsible for developing, presenting, and directing implementation of visions, missions, identities, philosophies, goals, and objectives of enterprises. If those leadership components and support are missing, then there may be no real context within which facilities—or facilities management programs—can be developed.

Most corporate executives strive for the development of organizations that have the potential to ultimately become leaders in their respective industries. Usually they know that accomplishing those lofty visions will require establishment of physical settings that will have the potential for being seen as visibly and positively as other current leading organizations in their respective industries are seen.

One co-author of this book is a veteran member of the Board of Directors of a national banking organization. He participated recently in many decision-making processes leading to the construction of a new bank headquarters building, a totally integrated workplace environment for that national bank. If any new banking organization hopes to compete with Wells Fargo, Bank One, Fifth-Third Bank, Community First, or other major banking organization, it will be important to develop facilities that have the look, feel, prestige, image, amenities, features, and aura of those major banking industry leaders and competitors.

The other co-author of this book is currently a volunteer leader in a growing church organization that is seeking to expand a church-operated school as well as to extend the outreach of its worship facilities. To a substantial extent, if this church is to attract students to the church's school and daycare operation or add to the church's membership, it will be important to develop facilities that have the positive characteristics of other leading churches within the area community.

If an attorney establishing a law practice or any group of attorneys seeking to establish a large law firm to compete with other major law firms, it will be important to develop law office facilities that have the features and aura of other leading law firms operating within those geographic areas. Traditionally, physical aspects of law firm workplace environments have proven to be important factors in recruiting both talented new law school graduates as well as veteran attorneys. Facilities can make huge differences in the ability to recruit and retain the best of personnel who are available or who may become available to organizations.

These banking, school and church, and law firm examples illustrate the impact and importance of senior leaders' visions and plans for organizations and the cultures that are envisioned and essentially required for the success of those organizations. The adage that "when in Rome, do as the

Romans do" has been around for a long time and bears both remembering and challenging when totally integrated workplace design and management is undertaken today.

## Tighten the Connections between Senior Leaders and Facilities Management

3M Company experienced so much growth and development throughout the 1950s, 60s, 70s, and early 80s that senior management decided major facilities expansions were needed and warranted. More specifically, the marketing organizations of some electronic products divisions were so geographically removed from obvious markets that senior management decided to act. Decisions were made in the mid-1980s to relocate some major business segments to the emerging high-technology center of Austin, Texas.

This strategic decision was driven by several business factors that included bringing 3M operations and people closer to customers and "into the same playground as other big playmates." 3M leaders sought to extend the image, positioning, and status of the corporation within those industry segments. There was also a strong desire to conserve some major company facilities at 3M Center in St. Paul for growth of other corporate operations.

A result of these 3M senior leadership decisions was a request for Facilities Management to "figure out how we can move these major business segments to the Austin, Texas area." A major goal was to accomplish this move as quickly as reasonably possible, which meant that there was not going to be time to plan and construct all new buildings and facilities.

Consequently, 3M Facilities Management and it's partners sought, found, leased, renovated, equipped, and conditioned available properties in Austin to make them appropriate for business operations being relocated from St. Paul. The requirement for speed in this situation necessitated leasing and renovating space to achieve totally integrated workplaces while new buildings and facilities were planned and constructed. Expiration of leases was timed to coincide with the dates on which newly-constructed corporate facilities could be occupied.

This scenario allowed 3M Facilities Management to respond to the strongly expressed strategic plans of senior management that included the enhancement of 3M's presence in Austin as quickly as possible. Ultimately,

3M Facilities Management accomplished the establishment of permanent owned buildings and facilities that continued 3M's high-level traditions of providing totally integrated workplace design and management.

Tightening the connections between senior management and facilities management programs in all organizations needs to be an on-going process. Critical components of that process are essential two-way commitments. Senior leaders, if they genuinely want totally integrated and well-managed workplaces that are appropriate for their organizations, must then make appropriate commitments to establish funding, staffing, and support of facilities management programs. Facilities managers must make commitments to senior management to develop high-performance programs capable of delivering facilities management outcomes and services that are coordinated with organizational strategic plans and that are confidently expected by senior management.

Sprint Corporation is headquartered in a Kansas City suburb. The corporation experienced phenomenal growth during the late 1980s and early 1990s. As a result, company growth necessitated significantly expanding its workforce. Immediate facilities requirements compelled Sprint to lease numerous properties at various dispersed geographic locations around the greater Kansas City area. Dispersal of company personnel into several geographic locations that were some distances from each other resulted in the company needing extensive transportation of mail, packages, shipping and receiving functions, food, and other support resources between and among facilities.

A natural outcome of this situation was money spent to connect the geographically-dispersed facilities via telecommunications, computer networks, mail transportation and management systems, extensive pickup and delivery routes, and related logistical methods. It soon became clear that running a dynamic company from many buildings in many different locations not only caused logistical nightmares but also was accelerating costs beyond acceptable levels. Maintaining desired corporate cultures, values, objectives, and desired approaches to work accomplishment also proved to be difficult to sustain.

The ultimate solution was the senior management strategic decisions to consolidate operations into a single campus site and to construct facilities required for corporate operations. Doing that required completing necessary demographic studies, scouting for potential sites, site acquisition, securing of associated development permits, and conceptualizing potential campus configurations. Also included were architectural and engineering planning, converting those plans into specific designs, developing budgets and proposals, gaining management approvals, construction, conditioning of spaces, occupying, and utilizing those facilities.

This Sprint experience can be regarded as a successful classic example of an extensive corporate strategic business plan supported by well-coordinated totally integrated workplace design and management processes. Sprint's senior leadership and corporate facilities management professionals collaborated and combined their visions, managerial wisdom, knowledge, experience, and determination to result in high-performance facilities for the company.

Another exciting example that emphasizes the importance and value of tight connections between an organization's senior management and an organization's facilities management professionals comes from 3M Company. Major accomplishments in both corporate strategic planning and in the development of totally integrated and managed workplaces were achieved for 3M's collection of divisions that provide products to the health-care industry.

3M senior management's strategic planning initiatives evolved to an objective of consolidating 3M health care divisions and component support units into a single corporate geographic location. The result of that objective was the development and construction of a new 500,000 square foot office building that was attached to two existing research buildings. This new facility enabled the company's health-care related businesses to consolidate all functions including research, engineering, sales and marketing, finance, human resources, and related functions into a complex of physically interconnected buildings that were adjacent to one another.

The ability to have auditoriums, cafeterias, corridors, meeting rooms, reception areas, parking lots, and other spaces jointly used by associates in affiliated departments fostered improved personnel communication and interaction and resulted in improved esprit-de-corps, collaboration, and work accomplishment. People worldwide have benefited from use of 3M's myriad of health care products. 3M experienced increased profits from this segment of business as a result of the combined efforts of 3M's senior corporate leadership and the professionals in 3M's Facilities Management Department. This is another 3M example of how "the whole became greater than the sum of its individual parts."

## Senior Management Can Remove Barriers to Quality Facilities Management

One of the most important roles that senior management can play is that of running interference and removing barriers to the advancement of plans for totally integrated workplace development and management. In many organizations, there are substantial amounts of resistance to change, incidences of turf protection, political posturing, well-intentioned but sometimes misdirected efforts of middle-level leaders, and undue concerns about status symbols. All of these situations can individually or collectively form barriers to high-performance totally integrated workplace development and management.

It is often very lonely at the top. Inevitably, senior leaders in all organizations will face tough challenges that ultimately requires their strength of character, convictions, good decision making capacities, and their determination to resolve these challenges. Because workplace development and management impacts on personnel at all levels within organizations, there are always facilities and workplace decisions that become unpopular to some.

Some people will disagree with facilities decisions that may range from the geographic location of their divisions, location of personal workspaces, arrangements of workstations, and to the color of their carpeting. While members of senior management cannot be routinely bothered with lower-level and sometimes trivial issues, they can—through their strong on-going overall commitment to totally integrated workplace design and management—pave the way for facilities management programs and professional facilities managers to function. Senior leaders are uniquely positioned to remove barriers to progress and success.

## The Power of Benchmarking

A benchmark can be defined as a standard or point of reference in measuring or judging quality, value, and relevancy. Benchmarking is the process used in business, industry, government, and other entities for gathering operational data from peer-type organizations for purposes of comparison, judging quality, measuring value, developing best practices, and determining relevancy.

The authors of this book, during their combined 75+ years of real-world business and professional experiences, have yet to meet any senior leader who didn't aspire to have her or his organization be "the best in class." No senior executive has ever admitted while conversing on a tee box or in the fitness center that she or he really didn't care if their organization was keeping pace with state-of-the-art industry precedence and practices. Neither have senior leaders expressed that they were willing to be second best (unless they knew they were currently third best or lower). Senior leaders want their organizations to be the best.

At 3M Company, the Facilities Management Department had routinely sought benchmarking partners that were peer-level organizations based on size, scope, complexity, and had similar markets (but were not significant competitors). 3M sought benchmarking partners that had campus settings, comparable work environments, and other similarities. During the timeframe of the early 1990s, as an outcome of relationships established through IFMA membership and participation in international conferences, the 3M Facilities Manager connected with counterpart facilities managers in several peer-level companies. On a formally scheduled basis, benchmarking meetings were held at peer-company locations resulting in each participant benefiting from tours, examples, discussions, and sharing of best practices.

The Coca-Cola Company, ConAgra, DuPont, Hallmark Cards, S. C. Johnson and Sons, Monsanto, and Sprint were companies with whom relationships were established with 3M's Facilities Management Department. Benefits to 3M included an expanding network of major organization facilities managers literally being on call; shared "war stories" of the great, good, bad, and ugly experiences; shared success stories; and current-to-the-moment industry and workplace statistics. Standards for space allocation, workstations, maintenance programs, environmental programs, compliance issues, security systems and processes, costs of operations, and other facilities management components were shared and discussed. And, highly valued long-term relationships resulted from that professional networking.

The ultimate value to 3M's senior management included periodic facilities management briefings and updates about the company's relative positioning and comparisons with peer-level organizations. It is highly probable, based on senior management feedback to the 3M Facilities Manager at that time, that their comfort level and overall appreciation for the company's facilities management program were elevated. In total, the close and tight connections between 3M's senior management and the

Facilities Management organization resulted in multiple positive outcomes related to totally integrated workplace design and management. Most important were all of the benefits that resulted for 3M personnel at all levels.

## *Summary*

Engaging senior management in facilities management endeavors is critical to the success of totally integrated workplace design and management. Real-world reality is that if senior management decides to make something a high priority, it gets approved, funded, staffed, and accomplished. On the other hand, if senior management does not seem to care about whether or not something is undertaken or accomplished, then progress will be difficult. Organization-wide and centrally-managed facilities management programs should be established by authorizing board action to be permanent on-going programs within organizations. For achievement of maximum impact, placement of facilities management programs should be as high as possible in organizational structures.

The individuals selected to be facilities managers will always be of major importance to the development of high-performance facilities management programs. Qualifications for the position of Facilities Manager should include an appropriate academic background, demonstrated work experience with facilities management responsibilities, and obvious aspirations to be professional facilities managers. Many organizations now recruit Certified Facility Managers (CFMs) or state "CFM preferred" when seeking professional facilities managers.

Establishment of a Facilities Planning and Utilization Committee is highly recommended as an integral part of facilities management programs. Membership should include members of organizations' senior management as well as representatives from the divisions, departments, agencies, branches, or units that make up organizations. Assessments of current facilities management situations, collective identification of needs, prioritizing those needs, and lending strong support and credibility to facilities management programs can be accomplished through these committees.

Senior leaders in organizations, if they genuinely want totally integrated and well-managed workplaces appropriate for their organizations, must make strong commitments to facilities management programs. In return, facilities managers must make commitments to senior management to develop state-of-the-art programs capable of delivering facilities management outcomes that are coordinated with the strategic plans of entire organizations. Examples of successes achieved through these partnerships in large organizations include 3M Company, Sprint, and many others. Consistent benchmarking by facilities managers with counterparts in peer-level organizations can also result in learning from others and continually evolving best practices that can be utilized in achieving totally integrated workplace design and management.

# Chapter 4
## *COMPONENTS OF HIGH-PERFORMANCE FACILITIES MANAGEMENT PROGRAMS*

### *Recommended Components for High-Performance Facilities Management Programs*

The scope and content of successful organization-wide facilities management programs devoted to totally integrated workplace design and management varies from program to program in both the private and public sectors as well as from small to large organizations. Many smaller corporate, private, governmental, not-for-profit, professional practices, and other organizations have no formalized facilities management programs at all.

Other smaller organizations may have someone designated as the Facilities Manager, but only view that responsibility as one of many duties for which that individual is responsible. Many midsize and larger organizations have placed well educated and specifically prepared facilities management professionals in higher-level leadership positions.

Establishment of facilities management programs should be accomplished, ideally, following the development of strategic plans for organizations followed by the development of strategic plans for facilities management and with those plans carefully coordinated with each other. Formally established ongoing programs typically are included as line items in budgets and have funding provided for continued program staffing even though personnel changes may occur.

### *Elements and Framework Recommended for Facilities Management Programs*

Five major elements combine to be a recommended framework for the development of organization-wide centrally-managed totally integrated workplace design and management programs (facilities management programs). These five major elements are supported by approximately thirty-two "stakeholder components" which provide the specialized knowledge, expertise, and experience necessary for successful program development. The five major elements are:

## *People, Place, Process and Technology*

IFMA defines facility management as "a profession that encompasses multiple disciplines to ensure functionality of the built environment by integrating people, place, process and technology" (IFMA website at www.ifma.com). PEOPLE, PLACE, PROCESS, and TECHNOLOGY have been presented, discussed, and stressed as four key elements of facilities management processes by IFMA for many years through the association's courses, publications, conferences, seminars, and training.

Thousands of facilities management professionals have learned how essential these elements are to the success of totally integrated workplace design and management. They are routinely conceptually integrating them into the day-to-day administration of their facilities management programs.

## *Add "Information"*

"Information" consists of data and facts that are acquired in any way and that are processed into meaningful contexts to become knowledge. Information does not mean validity, because inaccurate information may be gathered along with accurate information. Correct, accurate, and valid information is the basis for meaningful thinking, decision making, and the basis for taking actions of some kind. In workplaces, information is both the raw material for decision making and the performance of work as well as being a product of administrative and other processes used for work accomplishment.

Information is an essential and critical resource that needs to be professionally managed throughout the information cycle of creation, reception, collection, processing, distribution, use, storage, retrieval, retention, or elimination. Records are recorded information, regardless of medium or characteristics, that have been created within or received by an individual or organization and that have been or are being used as a basis for making decisions, accomplishing work, or as evidence of activities collectively described by the information contained within them. Practically speaking, today—in the eyes of the law—if recorded information exists on any media, it can be subpoenaed and will be considered a record.

## *People, Place, Process, Technology, Information*

The collective experience of this book's authors has evolved conceptually to now include five key elements known to be essential for totally integrated workplace design and management (high-performance facilities management). These five elements are people, place, process, technology, and information. The addition of information as a critical element is essential because again, some information is the raw material for decision making and the performance of work. Other information is the product of administrative and other processes used for the accomplishment of work.

Some information is usually an input to the performance of work while some other information is usually the output from the performance of work. There are legal, economic, conceptual, and practical reasons supporting the contention that information, which is the basis for knowledge, must be managed professionally and effectively if individuals and organizations are to survive and thrive. Information has become an essential element in the development of totally integrated workplace design and management.

## *A Whole Look at People, Information, Process, Technology, Place*

The authors have elected to discuss the five major elements in the order of people, information, process, technology, and place that combine to be a recommended framework for the development of high-performance facilities management programs. People are always the most important, most valued, and most expensive resource. Information is an essential input and raw material for any activities or work to take place. Some types of processes are necessary to transform inputs into outputs, and the requirements of those processes influences technology selection. Work spaces and workplaces should always be designed around the work to be done rather than to have expensive people change effective ways of doing things in order to conform to the constraints of inflexible facilities.

## People

Human life is precious. Nothing is more valuable or meaningful than the lives of people. People should always be regarded as the most essential, valuable, and precious resource. Parents are children's most essential, valuable, and precious resources. Children should also be the most essential, valuable, and precious resources to parents. Spouses should be each other's most essential, valuable, and precious resource. Great friendships are essential, valuable, and precious resources. Employees and personnel of organizations are those organizations' most essential, valuable, and precious resources.

As a result, virtually anything that can be done as part of totally integrated workplace design and management and that makes possible and compliments high-quality human endeavor will collectively benefit every one of the people involved as well as entire organizations. People are the dominant elements in all environments; and from them comes the thinking, accumulated knowledge, decision making, and actions necessary for survival and the advancement of civilization.

Animals act and react primarily based on instincts. In contrast, people act and react primarily because of conscious decisions made after gathering, assimilating, thinking, processing, concluding, translating information into knowledge, and ultimately acting in some way or ways. These tremendous and awesome human capacities are what truly distinguishes people and then places them at the top of all priorities over any other things.

## Information

One of the co-authors of this book continues to be alive today because some critical and current-to-the-moment information enabled saving his life. While flying as a minimally-qualified trainee co-pilot in the cockpit of a four-passenger aircraft alongside a VFR (visually rated only) pilot, inaccurate weather information received by radio coupled with poor flying decisions led them into an immense series of thunderheads at dusk and into a total blackout situation. Only their collective determination to focus entirely on the aircraft instrument panel turn-and-bank indicator and altimeter enabled them to maintain the altitude and control that was necessary to fly through the storm to eventual safety. Sometimes, inaccurate information leads to potential disasters while accurate and current-to-the moment information saves lives.

Organizations large and small can also die or live based on the information that comes to them or is eventually made available to them. Bad information can lead to creating products people do not need and will not buy or to poor quality services or products that drive more people away. Bad information used by senior leaders can result in creating businesses that could be doomed to failure or to other decisions that ultimately prove to be wrong. Bad information can cause failures to be in legal compliance resulting in adverse legal consequences including fines or imprisonment. More devastating might be the loss of organizational image, prestige, position, integrity, and trust.

Great information, on the other hand, can be incredibly powerful and valuable—literally a basis for continued life of individuals or organizations. Good information means good business. Good information leads to the creation of desirable and high-quality products and services. Good information leads to good marketing of products and services to high-potential customers and other people to be served. Good current-to-the-moment information in the minds of senior leaders can result in decision making that is consistently appropriate, accurate, practical, and that leads to high probabilities of continued success.

Arguably, information—as a key element of totally integrated workplace design and management—warrants consideration close in importance to the priority that must always be given to people. Remember that any one of these five elements must always be considered for their individual importance while never forgetting that real power comes from integrating the five of them in combination.

## Process

A "process" is a particular method of doing something that generally involves a number of steps or operations. Processes are multiple actions done in meaningful sequences to accomplish more complex, larger, and multi-faceted outcomes. Whether it was an author of this book constructing his family's home of logs and rock or airport control towers monitoring locations of multiple aircraft in the sky, individual processes and multiple processes performed in sequence were or are necessary to accomplish those objectives.

Dan Brathal first scouted Wisconsin forests to select trees that were harvested to be logs for their new home. A concrete foundation was poured before large rocks could be crafted into a magnificent fireplace. One step at a time, many steps in sequence, many sequences over time, and a wonderful structure was the result.

Today's manufacturing plants require scientifically created spaces and workplaces developed by highly technical architectural, engineering, and related work that is performed to achieve extremely close tolerances. Today's department stores require scientifically created spaces arranged to display products in the most appealing ways and place them in relation to other products likely to sell with them in combinations. Today's major office complexes require office designers, architects, space planners, users, facilities managers, and other stakeholder components working in combination to achieve office settings where information can be processed through its cycle to produce desired decisions and information outputs. Effective workplace design and management must support processes performed in the workplace.

## *Technology*

"Technology" can be defined as any manual, automated, or mental process generally using applied sciences to transform inputs into products or services. Each operation has a technology, even if it is manual. In society today, most people tend to think of technology in terms of physical tools or items of some type. Hammers, scalpels, drills, cables, pens, pencils, computers, phones, copiers, printers, heart pacemakers, airliners, and semi-trucks are all examples of technologies available for our selection and use.

Because technology is evolving and changing so rapidly and because of so many technologies available, it is more important than ever for facilities managers to make intelligent, informed decisions about automation. The stakes are high because such choices affect the human as well as technical aspects of operations. Job satisfaction and positive employee attitudes can be maintained only if technology selection, implementation, and change is managed well.

The right technological choices must be integrated with both senior management's strategic plans for organizations and with facilities managers' and other operations managers' strategic plans. Leaders and managers in today's global economy must be alert to all opportunities for improvement, and rapid changes in technology make it a particularly important area for continued evaluation.

Facilities managers have multiple interests and concerns regarding technology and its selection and use. Facilities management professionals need technology for purposes of construction design and space layout planning (CAD-CAM systems). They need environmental control and management systems, accounting and related administrative systems, and—depending on their industry—technologies common to and potentially unique to that industry.

Infrastructure requirements will include providing fiber-optic, coaxial, and wire cabling; computer servers; telephone closets; uninterrupted (UPS) and auxiliary power supplies; and conduits installed throughout facilities. All of these technology factors combine to make the element of technology fundamental to totally integrated workplace design and management.

## *Place*

A "place" can be broadly defined as anywhere on earth identifiable through GPS systems or anywhere in the universe that has been charted and mapped. More narrowly, a place is usually considered to be a particular region, area, location, or spot devoted to a specific purpose. Homes are places to live, theatres are places for entertainment, baseball stadiums are places to play or watch baseball, factories are places to manufacture things, and offices are places to transform information inputs into knowledge, decisions, and information outputs.

Of the five major elements critical to totally integrated workplace design and management, the element of place is discussed last of the five in this book—but certainly not because it is least important. It is presented and discussed last of the five because it is within appropriately developed spaces and workplaces that all of the five elements come together and interact to result in successful workplace environments. This scenario is equally applicable to the development of high-quality living quarters, excellent centers for doing business, good manufacturing plants, adequate centers for providing health care services, effective educational settings, centers of government, excellent office environments, and facilities that meet the needs of all kinds of organizations.

Excellent facilities will not guarantee organizations' success, and poor facilities will not guarantee organizations' failures. The same can be said about senior management, management at all levels, technologies, equipment, and employees. By themselves, none of these elements of any organization will be enough to ensure success. They are all parts of integrated workplaces, and to function effectively all parts must work together effectively. They are all interdependent parts of high-performance facilities management programs.

## *Thirty-Two Stakeholder Components*

Thirty-two stakeholder components support the five major elements that make up a recommended framework for high-performance facilities management programs. From these stakeholder components come the knowledge, expertise, experience, precedence, and bases necessary to create high-quality workplace environments. These stakeholder components are presented alphabetically rather than in any suggested order of importance. The list is extensive but should not be viewed as being all-inclusive. The level of importance and participation of each stakeholder often changes from project to project and organization to organization.

*Architecture.* The science and art of the architectural profession is among the most obvious and most important components of totally integrated workplace design and management. Architects usually participate in site selections, collaborate in analyzing and articulating organizational needs for facilities, design structures, collaborate during construction, inspect and approve construction processes, and accomplish related functions. They are key collaborators especially in the early stages of workplace definition, design, development, and construction—or in renovation of existing facilities. Their contributions include development of broad conceptual designs, which then will be translated, in collaboration with other stakeholders, into specific renovation or construction designs and specifications.

*Audio and Visual Services.* Most organizations will ultimately require facilities appropriate for use in providing varying kinds and levels of management, employee, customer, and other training, education, and interaction. Audio and visual services specialists usually participate in deciding what dimensions meeting facilities should be and what AV technology will be needed to fit various applications. They will also help develop specifications for electrical supplies, cabling systems necessary to enable use of presentation equipment, heating and cooling requirements, acoustical specifications, and closely related features.

*Business Continuity Planning.* Business continuity planning specialists should work with facilities managers and others to determine, verify the existence of, and develop business continuity plans. In larger organizations, these specialists should coordinate plans with multiple client divisions, branches, agencies, or units to assure that business continuity plans are developed, standardized as much as possible, and are carefully documented. Often included will be the selection of software used for plan development and documentation.

Collaboration with organizations' records managers and IT managers for purposes of collectively identifying and protecting vital records and information is always essential. Included in business continuity planning may be the development of portfolios of leasable or otherwise available empty spaces existing within close geographic distances to present facilities. The purpose of these portfolios is to be prepared in the event of terrorism, natural or human-created disasters, or other upset events which may necessitate an organization quickly needing to secure appropriate spaces and workplaces for operations and personnel.

Additional responsibilities of business continuity planners should be to collaborate with representatives of client organizations (divisions, departments, agencies, branches, and units) to carefully identify and specify what resources they would need in the event that interruption of business or operations occurred. Business continuity planning specialists function in both analysis and consulting roles to assist user groups as well as facilities managers and others when needed to maintain continual operations capabilities.

*Civil Engineering.* Civil engineering is the branch of professional engineering that typically focuses on the design of highways, bridges, tunnels, waterworks, harbors, and related structures. Virtually every building that is constructed must be accessible through some type or types of transportation networks such as streets, highways, or freeways.

Civil engineering is also typically responsible for specifying traffic control systems, signs, directional signs, parking lots, pavement and parking lot striping, and other things that generally bring order to pedestrian and vehicle transportation patterns and systems. Contributions of these very specialized engineering personnel are especially significant stakeholder components of high-performance facilities management programs.

***Community Agencies (Law Enforcement, Fire, Paramedics, Emergency Responders).*** Every facility that is constructed, renovated, and occupied must be designed and built to specifications that are required for conformance to building codes, fire codes, insurance regulations, and other specifications. In order for occupancy permits to be issued, such codes must be followed and construction methods approved by building code officials and fire officials. All facilities must also be accessible to community agency emergency responders when necessary.

When community agencies are responding to an upset condition, they want to know how buildings are built, what kinds of fire protection systems are in place, what kinds of materials may be hazardous and where they are located, and what other hazardous materials may be stored within properties. Facilities managers and representatives from these community agencies must collaborate periodically on the design, specification, construction, and occupancy of all organizations' facilities.

***Construction.*** Construction planning, management, and actual construction activities are among the most obvious and most important components of totally integrated workplace design and management. Construction methods must follow specifications in order to ensure integrity of buildings, verify that their operating systems are installed correctly, verify that code compliance is current and complete, and thus contribute to ongoing effectiveness of places for people to perform work. The ongoing collaboration between construction specialists, facilities managers, and other stakeholder components is essential to the development of high-quality workplaces.

***Custodial Services.*** Custodial services professionals should participate in developing specifications for external and internal surfaces and finishes. These surfaces and finishes may include floors, ceilings, restroom fixtures, counter tops, sinks, partitions, mirrors, windows, and related structural elements that custodians will ultimately be responsible for cleaning and maintaining. Another major custodial responsibility is typically garbage, refuse, and trash collection and disposition. The expertise and experience of custodial professionals should be integrated into the planning, design, and specification development for all facilities.

***Electrical Engineering.*** Electricity supplies are obviously essential resources for the operation of facilities that require any amount of electricity. The tremendous dependence on electricity for modern-world facilities necessitates its availability and appropriate distribution. Electrical engineers provide the knowledge, expertise, and specific direction necessary to assure that adequate amounts of power will be provided when it is needed, where it is needed, and through systems to which requesters for power can connect.

Electrical engineers should also participate in the coordinated planning necessary to minimize power outages and be prepared to provide alternative sources of power in the event of terrorism, natural, or human-created disasters. Many U. S. and Canadian East Coast electrical engineering professionals have recently devoted substantial amounts of time to resolving issues that led to the great Northeastern U. S. and Southeastern Canada blackout of August, 2003. Facilities managers, absent a partnership with electrical engineers, would not be able to provide useful facilities without the inclusion of adequate and appropriate supplies of electricity.

***Environmental Engineering.*** Given ongoing concerns for environmental protection, it is imperative that environmental engineering professionals partner with facilities managers in the design and construction of environmentally friendly facilities. Recognizing the potential for environmental mishaps along with the potential for heavy fines and other penalties, emission control systems, hazardous materials spill containment, storm water runoff containment, and air quality monitoring and specifications development are among the major contributions made to totally integrated workplace design and management.

***Facilities Management.*** Professional facilities managers should provide the leadership and direction for organization-wide centrally-managed facilities management programs. Facilities managers should be the focal points and principal leaders in achieving the effective combination, installation, and utilization of essential elements and stakeholder components necessary to result in high-performance facilities management programs.

***Finance.*** Workplaces cost money. Finance departments or units within organizations are typically responsible for coordinating the financial planning, administration, and management necessary for organizations to function. Facilities management programs and facilities managers need to have strong allies among senior financial leaders of organizations. Extraordinarily close communications, collaboration, and cooperation will be essential if the strategic business plans of organizations are to be meshed with facilities management strategic planning. They need to result in financial resources being available at appropriate levels when needed. Financial leaders are also important allies because they often are highly instrumental in determining organization-wide spending priorities.

*Food Services.* People like to eat. Whenever it is determined that food is to be made available within facilities, then food services professionals should be consulted relative to appropriately providing that food. Facilities ramifications of food services decisions include how food services areas are designed, constructed, equipped, and maintained. Building codes, health codes, sanitation requirements, OSHA requirements, and related concerns must always be identified and addressed. You can not just whip out a charcoal grill and throw on the steaks—especially if the facility happens to be the Empire State Building or the Sears Tower. Facilities managers must act quickly when they smell the barbecue sauce!

*Grounds Maintenance.* The grounds surrounding any building or complex provide settings for those facilities and also play important roles in projecting images of quality and success for organizations. The old adage that "you can tell something about a man by the suits he wears" also applies to organizations. You can learn some things about organizations by how the grounds surrounding their facilities are planned, designed, manicured, equipped, and maintained. Landscape designers, for example, are often called on to create aesthetically pleasing and prestige enhancing grounds surrounding facilities. Grounds maintenance specialists and their expertise and experience are important to totally integrated workplace design and management.

*Information Technology.* Computers, computer peripherals, telephone and other communications systems, infrastructure technologies and connections, and related technologies are now essential for successful operations in virtually all organizations. In fact, "intelligent buildings," discussed in Chapter 7 of this book, are literally being constructed around information technology architectures that were determined to be essential for work performance in some organizations.

As many of the essential technology components as possible should ideally be built into structures at the times they are constructed. CIOs (chief information officers), IT (information technology) managers, MIS (management information systems) managers and other IT specialists should collaborate with facilities managers as essential stakeholder components to achieve totally integrated workplace design and management.  Chapter 9 of this book is devoted to the topic of facilities planning for information and technology systems.

*Interior Design.*  Interior designers should work closely with facilities managers in order to collaborate in the planning, design, arrangement, configuration, equipping, environmental conditioning, and accenting of efficient, effective, and aesthetically pleasing workplaces.  Careful consideration must always be given to the selection of surfaces and finishes that will have high probabilities of easy maintenance and long-term durability.

Just because something looks nice, that does not mean it will be easy to maintain or that it will last a long time.  There are many quality university-level and private schools of interior design that are preparing highly creative and skilled interior designers.  Their knowledge, creativity, and expertise coupled with that of professional facilities managers results in powerful combinations of talent beneficial to achieving totally integrated workplace design and management.

*Mail Services.*  Mail services specialists develop expertise in the planning, design, arrangement, equipping, staffing, and operations of mail processing facilities.  In organizations of substantial size in particular, mail services specialists will be key individuals in planning and placing mail rooms as well as mail stops (mail distribution and pickup locations) within divisions, departments, or operating units.  The contributions of mail services specialists are many.

*Maintenance.*  The authors of this book grew up on farming and ranching operations, one in Wisconsin and one in North Dakota.  Each worked closely with a wonderful father and from early boyhood repeatedly heard and learned that when it comes to farm implements and equipment, "oil and grease make cheap repairs."  And, those astute fathers were correct.  Preventive maintenance coupled with continuing vigilance to identify and fix situations where maintenance is needed results in many savings of resources.

Maintenance specialists should also be consulted by facilities managers for their expertise during planning stages of facilities projects.  Their input can be incredibly valuable in designing and specifying building operating systems and equipment.  They usually know what consistently performs at design specifications, what tends to fail more often, and usually know what is easier to repair and maintain.  Many maintenance specialists are uniquely knowledgeable about systems, equipment, and product brands that are better candidates to purchase and use than others due to their records of performance, durability, and maintainability. The systems and equipment that tenants rely on should be selected in collaboration with facilities management and maintenance professionals.

**Mechanical Engineering.** The knowledge of mechanical engineering professionals is often the most sought-after expertise in facilities management operations. For example, attend a professional conference at even the best conference centers or luxury hotels and the meeting rooms will often be perceived as either too warm or too cold. Workplace surveys show that the single most common complaint to facilities managers is about temperature levels, it is either too hot or too cold. Not infrequently, two employees who sit next to each other will communicate that one thinks it is too warm while the other says it is too cold.

Mechanical engineers are on the front lines in terms of needing to collaborate with facilities managers and other stakeholder components as needed to carefully plan facilities. Mechanical engineering programs should also be established as bases for quick responses to systems that malfunction or fail. Mechanical engineers are extremely valuable stakeholder contributors to high-performance facilities management.

**Medical, Industrial Hygiene, and Toxicology.** These highly skilled professionals are responsible for assuring that emergency medical response systems and equipment are available when and where they are needed. They also assist with the development of programs that work to assure appropriate levels of air quality containing minimum levels of air contaminants. Recommendations for air-handling systems, filtration systems, adequate air turnover rates, and making recommendations to minimize the development of molds, spores, bacteria, and harmful toxins result from the work of these specialists.

These professionals also monitor workplace conditions for purposes of identifying potential risks from long-term exposure to chemicals, irritants, and other potentially harmful substances that may negatively impact air quality and lead to employee discomfort or health problems. They should collaborate with facilities managers to assure that facilities are designed and operated in accordance with regulations and threshold limit values for contaminants. They are skilled partners in the development of totally integrated workplace design and management.

***Procurement.*** Procurement professionals are usually responsible for purchasing resources that they have been requested to purchase, for finding needed commodities and services, for determining which ones meet needed specifications, finding and negotiating best prices, and selecting appropriate sources from among available choices. They typically negotiate purchase agreements with selected sources and coordinate all aspects of transactions and acquisitions processes. Purchasing professionals should collaborate with facilities management professionals in the identification and selection of needed commodities and services and to then negotiate best prices and appropriate purchase agreements.

***Public Affairs.*** Public affairs specialists typically interface with community agencies such as economic development agencies, government agencies, political organizations, and not-for-profit organizations. Contacts will be maintained with chambers of commerce, better business bureaus, other agencies, and the media to represent organizations to the public. Public affairs specialists should collaborate with facilities managers in the event of and when facilities-related issues arise or warrant attention by any or all of these constituents.

***Receptionists.*** In many organizations, receptionists are employed in part so that warm and professional welcomes will greet visitors. Professional receptionists with good interpersonal and communication skills can be valuable representatives of organizations who project desired organizational images and cultures to the public. Never underestimate the magnetism of a smiling face, a warm welcome, and the words "may we be of help to you." Facilities managers are usually responsible for planning, designing, locating, equipping, furnishing, and decorating places where receptionists are stationed.

***Records Management.*** Chapter 10 of this book is devoted to the importance of a partnership between facilities management and records management. Records on all media are the memory of organizations and the basis for being in either legally defendable or legally indefensible positions. Records must be professionally managed within all organizations if organizations are to be successful. There are many records management issues for which resolution has facilities management implications. Use the content of Chapter 10 as your basis for the development of organization-wide records and information management programs and systems and for understanding why records managers and facilities managers need to work closely together.

***Safety Engineering.*** Safety engineers are usually responsible for the assessment of workplace conditions, identification of existing or potential dangers and unsafe practices, and for prescribing solutions for those situations. Frequently, the solutions they recommend have direct impacts on facilities design, operations, and management. Sometimes their recommendations will relate to facilities design and the operation of building systems. Other times their suggested solutions will impact on current research and lab practices. Yet other recommendations will focus on maintenance procedures and practices. Obviously, all of these situations will require facilities management collaboration and participation in the implementation of solutions.

***Senior Management.*** Senior management support for facilities management programs and for facilities managers is critical to their success. Chapter 3 of this book is devoted to the topic of engaging senior management in facilities management endeavors. Use the content of that chapter as a basis for strengthening and solidifying the support of senior management for your facilities management programs.

***Security.*** Security professionals are usually responsible for providing protection against terrorism, protection for personnel to the greatest extents possible, protection for the facilities and resources of organizations, and for providing controlled access to facilities. Access control systems include closed-circuit camera monitoring systems, electronic door locks, pass readers, alarm/intrusion systems, and related items which all have facilities management implications. When there are upset events or disruptions, security personnel will participate in crowd control, traffic control, directing emergency responders, and overall security of those sites where events occur.

Security responsibilities typically include executive and senior leader protection and mitigation of organized crime and other illegal activities, especially outside of the United States and Canada. Security responsibilities typically include interacting with law enforcement agencies and conducting investigations of alleged employee fraud or breeches of ethics. Additionally, security professionals are occasionally involved with protection of personnel embroiled in domestic disputes or volatile relationships and related workplace security issues. Because many security solutions have facilities implications, security professionals should be key stakeholder components in the development of high-performance facilities management programs.

**Shipping and Receiving.** Shipping and receiving activities, depart-ments, and specialists need space and workplaces appropriate for perform-ance of those functions. Physical locations of buildings, loading docks, and other facilities are always important because of requirements to be accessible for deliveries by trucks, other motor vehicles, and sometimes by train. The design of receiving docks, lifting devices, security provisions for shipping and receiving functions, working spaces needed for loading and unloading activities, and related issues all have strong facilities manage-ment implications. As a result, shipping and receiving specialists are important stakeholder components of high-performance facilities manage-ment.

**Suppliers.** Often overlooked are the importance and value of supplier roles relative to planning, designing, constructing, renovating, equipping, supplying, and operating totally integrated workplaces. Suppliers provide their expertise through offering and presenting options for workplace design and management. Suppliers' input is important in the attainment of budget and spending objectives that are often responsibilities of facili-ties managers. Never underestimate what suppliers or potential suppliers may be willing to give away in terms of their expertise, consulting assis-tance, and sharing of information resources.

**Telecommunications.** Telecommunications specialists identify, spec-ify, assist in procuring, and assist in installing infrastructure equipment and systems that are necessary for supporting communications functions and activities. Facilities management often pays for infrastructure telecom-munications equipment and, as a result, should be involved in that plan-ning. Chapter 9 of this book is devoted to the topic of facilities planning for information and technology systems and includes content pertaining to the importance of a close working relationship between telecommuni-cations professionals and facilities managers.

**Tenants.** The customer is always right. Even if you know the cus-tomer is wrong, the customer still generally needs to be treated as though she or he is right. However, there is no other reason for facilities manage-ment programs to exist than to serve tenants. If there were no tenants in facilities there would be little or no need for facilities management pro-grams. Tenants are those who occupy spaces and workplaces and need to be viewed as customers or clients of facilities management programs. Thoughtful and caring relationships between tenants and facilities management personnel are keys to providing workplaces where tenants can perform their work effectively, efficiently, and in relative comfort.

***Transportation.*** In many facilities management situations—especially in larger organization campus settings—there are needs for transporting personnel, commodities, and other resources routinely from one facility to others. Shipping and receiving specialists work with facilities managers to design and create shipping and receiving facilities often based on requirements developed by owners of the transportation vehicles. Regulatory requirements for packaging, labeling, and manifesting certain materials (especially controlled substances) must be accommodated. Facilities managers need to work with transportation specialists or providers to make sure every effort is made to meet those regulatory requirements for the health and safety of all tenants.

***Utilities.*** Utilities refers to electricity, telephone, natural gas, fuel oil, water, and wastewater treatment. Facilities management professionals must interact with representatives of these utilities for purposes of collectively understanding what products and services are available from utility providers. Facilities management programs usually are responsible for forecasting and managing expenditures for utility commodities and services. As a result, utilities representatives combine to be important stakeholder components of high-performance facilities management programs.

## Summary

The scope and content of facilities management programs varies from program to program and organization to organization. Many smaller organizations have no formalized facilities management programs at all. Other smaller organizations may have someone designated as the facilities manager but only view that responsibility as one of many for which that individual is responsible. Many midsize and larger organizations have well-educated and specifically prepared professionals in leadership positions as facilities managers.

Historically, professional facilities management has been viewed conceptually as having four major components—people, place, process, and technology. The authors of this book strongly believe that a fifth component, information, should be added and become part of a recommended conceptual framework for the establishment of high-performance facilities management programs.

Information is the raw material for decision making and the performance of work. Some information is the product of administrative and other processes used for the accomplishment of work. Some information is the input to the performance of work while other information is the output of the performance of work.

People, information, process, technology, and place are the five major elements presented as a recommended conceptual framework for the establishment of totally integrated workplace design and management and for high-performance facilities management programs. People are always the most important and most expensive resource.

Information is essential for any activities or work to take place. Some processes are necessary to transform inputs into outputs, and the needs of those processes influences technology selection. Workspaces and workplaces should always be designed around the work to be done rather than to have expensive people change efficient ways of doing things simply to conform to the constraints of inflexible facilities.

Again, these five major elements of people, information, process, technology, and place combine to be a recommended framework for the development and operation of organization-wide centrally-managed facilities management programs. Additionally, the five major elements are supported by at least thirty-two stakeholder components that provide the specialized knowledge, expertise, and experience necessary for the development of high-performance totally integrated workplace design and management.

# Chapter 5
*ASSESSING YOUR ORGANIZATION'S CURRENT FACILITIES MANAGEMENT SITUATION*

## *Critique and Adjust Your Facilities Management Programs On an Ongoing Basis*

While many things are characteristic and true about business operations, change is one of the most common and most critical of those characteristics. Assessing the vitality of a business is at the center of what professional management is all about. If change were not both necessary and sometimes difficult, managing a business, a government entity, or other organization would be substantially less complicated and perhaps less challenging.

Why is change such a constant characteristic of business or organizational operations? One factor, among many others, that causes change is the continuing evolution of new products and services and the varying levels of demand for those products and services. Usability, quality, fit-for-purpose, durability, popularity, market penetration, and numerous other factors impact the success and ultimately the demand for specific products and services.

Production and delivery of products or services requires inputs (raw materials, information, skills, knowledge, and experience) and outputs (finished goods and saleable services). Because there are potentially many variables within the ingredients for inputs and outputs, it is critical that all of them are managed well, even while market conditions, technology, and process changes may be rapidly occurring. It is common that the necessary inputs and the outputs will impact the ultimate overall demand for products and services.

Physical products are a combination of materials that when combined in a prescribed way results in something that is more useful than the original materials used separately. Saleable services result from combining experience, knowledge, and skills that exist within a person or an entity at levels not possessed by other individuals or entities and therefore creating services that others are willing to buy in order to get that combination of experience, knowledge, and skill.

Variations and changes taking place in any of numerous factors should cause managers to recognize and assess those changes and to determine how those changes will effect, may effect, or are currently effecting the delivery of products or services. An important element of that assessment is to determine how the changes in business operations are likely to impact the need for potential facilities management responses and changes.

## Know Thyself, Thy Client, and Thy Current Situation

The facilities management process requires an ongoing understanding of the business or organizational elements and conditions for which facilities are designed, developed and managed to support. As business conditions change, facilities management programs may need to be changed in order to provide different or stronger methods of supporting business or other organizational operations.

Facilities management programs should be monitored on a continuous basis in order to assure that current-to-the-moment processes and programs exist to support current business and operational requirements. Performing a well-structured and continuous assessment of current facilities management practices is vital to the ongoing success of high-performance facilities management programs. Aside from the direct support of overall business and organizational objectives, there is no other useful or meaningful reason for facilities management programs to exist.

Facilities management program assessments should be performed in carefully structured and well-planned ways. Assessment of current practices is often done as part of ongoing strategic facilities planning exercises. While it is certainly appropriate to perform assessments during strategic planning, it is also important to monitor and adjust practices on an ongoing basis, if necessary, to more responsively and timely support changing business operations. Failures to conduct management process assessments, or assessments performed too infrequently, can result in facilities management programs evolving to be out of synchronization with and out of support for business and operating objectives.

No business endeavor would or should begin without gaining some understanding about anticipated levels of demand for the specific products or services provided by that endeavor. It logically follows that in order to provide meaningful and useful services, facilities management organizations must know as much about their clients as any business owner would need to know about her or his customers. Businesses usually are established only after performing thoughtful market research aimed at determining the viability and probability of success for proposed ventures.

Facilities management professionals should also research the ongoing needs of their clients and translate those needs into meaningful and useful portfolios of services that will have a high probability of satisfying the needs and best interests of their clients. Like doing market research, facilities management professionals should know and understand what their product (service) offerings should achieve for their clients. The product, facilities management services, must be as well defined and as well understood as any other products or services presented to any marketplace.

Business and operational conditions frequently vary from project to project, so facilities managers must also be prepared to adjust their services and to find solutions that appropriately respond to varying situations. In other words, standards are very important and very useful for most situations, but facilities management professionals must also be prepared to deviate from standards in efforts to provide the best overall solutions for their clients.

It is equally important for facilities managers to understand their clients' requirements and to seek solutions that are best suited to serve client needs as well as to serve overall organizational needs. It would be counterproductive for most facilities managers to force standard solutions onto clients if those standard solutions would not meet client requirements. Likewise, it would be counterproductive to prescribe solutions that fail to respect overall organizational objectives.

Facilities management professionals are challenged to provide solutions that address client requirements. Those requirements may be very different from what clients want or think they need. Many facilities managers become somewhat "caught in the middle" because they are faced with balancing client wants and perceived needs while striving to meet the greater needs of entire organizations. Services and product offerings must strike optimum balances that best serve individual clients as well as whole organizations.

## Develop Service Delivery Systems

Product (service) delivery systems must also be developed. It is useless to offer services if there are not effective ways to request and deliver those services. Whether it be a formal shop work order system, a work request system, a request for services, or some other device used to request services, there must be mechanisms and procedures made available for clients to request the help of facilities management organizations.

Work request systems initiate procedures whereby facilities management professionals become engaged in projects and arrange to address client requests. Effective service request and delivery systems are as critical to successful facilities management programs as they are to any organization offering products or services. It is critical that facilities managers, on an ongoing basis, assess, analyze, and understand how they are going to accomplish the request for and the delivery of their services.

Again, effective means of delivering services are very important to the success of facilities management programs. But, service does not end when specific projects are finished. Ongoing attention to client needs is also crucial. Additionally, clients must know how and where to quickly contact facilities management professionals. Unfortunately, human nature indicates that if clients are not attended to in ways they expect to be treated, they will often forget about all the good services they have received, but will quickly remember bad service experiences.

Constant vigilance and attention to communication practices assure that clients have effective access to the help they need and to the services they rely on to do their jobs well. A continuing assessment of client satisfaction will reveal where adjustments must be made in facilities management processes in order to assure constantly high-quality levels of client satisfaction.

## Do Not Leave High Levels of Service to Chance

It should never be assumed that provision of high-quality services will continue to remain the provision of high-quality services if left unattended. It cannot be assumed that current customer requirements will remain constant. And, it cannot be assumed that satisfied clients will remain satisfied clients if they are ignored. Additionally, it is dangerous to assume that processes and procedures used for delivering services will remain adequate for long periods of time if left unattended.

Key to the success of facilities management programs is the need for facilities management professionals to continuously monitor and know the business and operational conditions within their organizations. Facilities management professionals should use that knowledge to communicate with their clients in order to assure correct and current-to-the-moment understanding of client requirements.

## Change, Add, and Upgrade Services When Necessary

While it is necessary to monitor and assess the effectiveness of facilities management programs, it is equally important to make adjustments in those programs when appropriate. Changes are often very necessary in response to fluctuating business conditions, changing client requirements, and evolving technologies. Changes often will require more effective ways of performing facilities management transactions and meeting facilities management needs.

Trying to manage change and to adjust facilities management programs while businesses and other organizations are running along at today's pace is like "trying to nail Jell-O to the wall." Adjusting facilities management programs in appropriate and timely ways and in direct response to changing business environments is often extraordinarily challenging for facilities management professionals.

## Many Variables Must be Considered in Order to Support Strategic Plans

Many variables within organizations and facilities management programs must be monitored, assessed, and if necessary, be adjusted, added, deleted, or changed. Those variables include, among others, overall business objectives, corporate cultures, work processes, procedures, policies, and economic conditions. Regulatory requirements, market sizes and extents of penetration, supplier capabilities and performance, financial issues, human resources skills and capabilities, and many other variables must be considered. The following paragraphs highlight some of those areas that require continuous auditing, monitoring, and adjusting if and when necessary.

*First,* it is critical that facilities management professionals be aware of and familiar with organization, institution, agency, or other entities' strategic business plans. Strategic business plans typically include, among other contents, clear descriptions of organizations' products or services, identification of markets and customers, and perhaps visions and mission statements that include stated business values and operating principles.

Organizations' strategic business plans usually also contain human resources principles, short-term and long-term financial goals and objectives, and revenue and expenses forecasts. Also usually included are multiple-year forecasts for anticipated growth of existing and potential new markets, revenue, expenses, employees, and facilities. It is essential that facilities management programs be fully prepared to support organizations' strategic business plans.

**Second,** facilities management organizations must prepare and manage their own strategic facilities plans. Strategic facilities plans should include assessments of where facilities should be physically located in relation to organizations' customers, suppliers, and distribution networks (streets, roads, highways, railroads, waterways, and telecommunication networks used for delivering some services). Strategic facilities management plans should also identify how many locations and how many employees will need to be accommodated today and in the future.

**Third,** financial considerations should be assessed and applied to determine whether needed facilities should be owned or leased. Establishment of standards for space and workstations should be developed and promoted in order to accomplish reasonably accurate and reliable estimates of future space requirements along with the development of plans to address those requirements. It is critical that financial components of strategic facilities plans be continuously assessed and adjusted in order to remain current and in direct support of organization-wide business and operational objectives.

**Fourth,** facilities management organizations must be developed and operated with the accommodation of strategic facilities plans in mind. Development of effective facilities management organizations that are capable of managing and executing strategic facilities plans requires staffing plans that identify the skill sets needed to serve clients effectively. Effective organizations always need reporting structures that provide for the best possible communication channels and for the most direct routes to clients.

Expenses will always be incurred, and good organization plans should include forecasts of expenses along with well-designed processes for managing and accommodating those expenses. Ongoing operations planning and process control systems and procedures must also be developed in order to effectively achieve organizational operating goals and objectives. Facilities management organizations must be continuously assessed and operated in fluid and flexible ways that meet changing requirements of their clients.

*Fifth,* every effective facilities management organization is built on the foundation of well-conceived and well-executed business processes, procedures, standards and policies. As mentioned earlier in this chapter, successful facilities management organizations have in place efficient methods for clients to request services. Additionally, virtually every successful facilities management organization has in place efficient methods for delivering those services that effectively respond to client requests.

Whether it is a standard work order system that enables ordering and arranging internal services or that enables ordering and arranging for external contracted services, the means of response to and for satisfaction of client requests must be established. It is necessary that facilities management operating processes be developed, monitored, assessed, and adjusted as necessary to serve ongoing client requirements.

*Sixth,* many components, when thoughtfully and successfully integrated into total workplace designs, result in strong and effective high-performance facilities management programs. Spaces and services related to mail receiving, sorting, and delivery, to copy centers, to cafeterias and other food (vending) services, to records and information storage and retrieval, and to other support spaces and services are necessary components of effective workplace design and of high-quality facilities management programs.

The extent to which all of these and other workplace components are integrated will determine and measure the effectiveness of totally integrated workplaces. Telecommunications systems, shipping/receiving facilities, manufacturing material handling facilities, and office supply delivery and storage need to be carefully planned. Amenities such as sundry shops and barbershops among many others may be important ingredients in the operation of workplaces. All combine to enable workers to be as productive as their skills and attitudes allow them to be. It is important for facilities management professionals to continuously assess the value of such associated workplace components and to provide them in situations where employee productivity can be maximized by the provision of such services.

**Seventh,** space planning, allocation, design, finishing, furnishing, occupancy, and ongoing management are normally responsibilities of every high-performance facilities management program. Provisioning of space with heating, cooling, electricity, lighting, acoustic controls, and other systems is central to the day-to-day routine operation of facilities management programs.

Processes must be in place for the development of space and workstation standards and for the development of energy usage (heat, cooling, lights, and electricity) standards. Processes must also be established for the development of furniture standards and for space tracking and accounting systems. These processes require considerable human and technology interaction. Successful management of these processes requires routine assessments of their effectiveness, value, and efficiency.

## A Partial Summary At This Point

The operation of successful facilities management programs over extended periods of time requires continual market research. Know your products and services. Know your clients/customers. Have appropriate distribution systems in place. Provide outstanding service —regularly and consistently. Creatively monitor and adjust plans as needed. Strive to provide services and product offerings that strike optimum balances between client and organizational needs in order to meet the expressed needs of those constituents. Make sure that facilities management strategic plans always enable and complement the strategic plans of organizations.

## Eight...and Counting

**Eighth,** real estate processes must always be intelligently evolved, developed, and implemented and then continually monitored and adjusted as necessary. Portfolios should be developed that include an optimum mix of owned properties and leased properties in order to flexibly meet changing needs for facilities space.

Specific plans should be ready to acquire space when needed, and exit plans should be ready to enable reductions in space if needs to downsize materialize. There is always merit in being ready to rapidly get into facilities when more facilities are needed. And, there are economic and other benefits of being able to leave facilities when they are no longer required.

70

Information systems supporting good facilities management programs should include the development and maintenance of integrated real estate programs and space tracking systems.

*Ninth,* well-developed and carefully managed construction processes are especially critical. They are very important because of often-substantial costs involved along with other major issues such as building codes; health, safety, and environmental codes; and related challenges. Developing established architectural programs, established engineering programs, building design standards, specific construction programs, and accurate cost control systems all must integrate in order to have carefully managed construction processes.

Architectural programs include assuring structural integrity, appropriate sizing, high-quality aesthetics, essential facilities access, and other attributes that combine to develop appropriate facilities which reflect the images desirable for organizations. Engineering programs must include mechanical (heating, ventilation, and air-conditioning) systems; electrical systems; infrastructure systems such as streets, roads, parking; water supplies and sewers; landscaping; anticipation of and design for ongoing maintenance programs; and closely related functions.

Building design standards should include standards for amounts of space to be provided, optimum manufacturing components or office facilities, and sizing of work areas. Standards should be prepared for manufacturing settings, research labs, offices, conference rooms, and meeting facilities. Appropriate interior designs, integration of amenities such as convenience shops, food services, hair stylists, barber shops, banking services, and related functions should all be considered. The development of alternative groups of standardized manufacturing workstations, typical office workplaces, furniture and finishes; and for related workplace components should be specified.

Comprehensive construction programs should exist to include processes for ordering construction work; monitoring building or renovation progress; and for assuring compliance with architectural, design, and engineering specifications. Maintenance of construction accounting and information systems to accomplish construction accountability is always essential.

*Tenth,* state-of-the-art technology planning, implementation, and utilization processes are increasingly important in workplace environments where advanced technology use is usually essential for effective and efficient organizational development, competitiveness, and success. Development of leading-edge technology necessitates infrastructures that make selection, installation, operation, and continual upgrading of that technology possible.

Continuing assessment of infrastructure capabilities is obviously essential to achieving adequacy of technology implementation and use. Whether it is robotics use in manufacturing environments or computers and peripherals use in offices, the ongoing assessment of technology and its infrastructure has never been as important as it is now. Every indication is that this importance will accelerate in the future.

Technology design systems, infrastructure development plans, technology selection processes, technology integration scenarios, and related functions must be continually assessed and integrated with planning for total workplace development and management. Facilities management professionals must work closely with manufacturing technology professionals, information technology professionals, records managers, and other technologically-intensive work area colleagues to assure that well-coordinated monitoring and assessment takes place regularly and consistently.

*Eleventh,* current-to-the moment comprehensive security and safety processes are of paramount importance in an age of the war on terrorism. People need to know that they are protected, and they need to be assured often that their physical safety needs are uppermost in the thinking of their organizations' senior leadership. The regular assessment by facilities management professionals of the security and safety situation within organizations is one of the most important responsibilities of facilities and security management professionals.

Well-developed personnel safety programs and procedures, worker's compensation program reviews, facilities safety programs and procedures, and intellectual property security programs require continual assessment. Vital records identification and protection programs and related functions should all be routinely assessed and incorporated into well-developed operating standards and procedures.

*Twelfth,* regular assessments of environmental processes are especially important if organizations are to be fully capable of qualifying for necessary facilities-related occupancy, emissions, discharges, and other general environmental permits. Companies, businesses, government agencies at all levels, and other organizations all want to be welcomed within their respective communities. Achieving those objectives necessitates being good citizens and, among other things, meeting all community expectations relative to care of the environment.

Emergency procedures should also be in place to guide personnel of organizations relative to dealing with emergencies such as fires, floods, spills, emissions, and related potentially dangerous conditions. Assessing organizational readiness should also be directed to having disaster recovery procedures in place as integral parts of overall facility control systems. The abilities of organizations to respond to upset conditions tell surrounding neighbors about the commitment organizations have to being good environmental stewards and high-quality organizational citizens.

## *Summary*

While we have stated in other chapters of this book that people are the most important and expensive resource of any organization, reality is that facilities are usually organizations' second largest component of administrative expenses. Next to payroll (after paying the salaries, wages, and benefits of the people who do the work), facilities are almost always the next most expensive resource. Many organizations, unfortunately, have been squandering profits because of poorly established and ineffectively managed facilities programs.

Typically, a one dollar savings in facilities expenses can be the equivalent of generating ten dollars in sales revenue. Effective facilities management programs have historically achieved industry-wide cost reductions in the realm of 30 percent with no reduction of services. Those savings can be considered as direct contributions to the financial bottom line.

Such results have been achieved by consistently assessing organizations' current facilities management programs. Continual critiquing and adjusting of facilities management programs as discussed in this chapter should result in assuring high levels of client/customer satisfaction and in making multiple continuing contributions to the development of high-performance facilities management programs.

# Chapter 6

*WINNING STRATEGIES FOR QUALITY
FACILITIES MANAGEMENT*

## Tried-and-Proven Winning Strategies for Strengthening Or Developing Facilities Management Programs

The co-authors of this book each enjoyed exciting times (at least in their own minds) as high school athletes playing baseball and basketball—and each continues to compete to this day. Each learned at a very early age that knowing and executing the fundamentals of each game was the major requirement for competitiveness and success. We learned early in basketball that if a fellow player could not dribble a basketball down the court and make a lay-up, do not try to teach him the Auburn Shuffle—because it was not going to work! Defensively, if a guy could not move fast enough to play man-to-man defense and keep himself between an opponent and the basket, do not try to teach him the 1-3-1 trap defense—because it was not going to work either!

"Fundamentals first" is an axiom that applies to each and every discipline and profession. And so it is in professional facilities management. What is needed most in today's organizations—whether they are small, midsize, large, huge, private, public, not-for-profit or other—is knowledge and application of the fundamentals of high-quality facilities management as a base for organization-wide facilities management programs to be successful.

Chapter 1 defined and explained "facilities management" as fundamental for total workplace design and management. Chapter 2 discussed the critical integration of elements necessary for high-quality workplaces. Chapter 3 discussed how to secure and maintain senior management support and support of personnel at all levels. And, Chapter 4 presented the components of successful facilities management programs.

Chapter 5 focused on assessing your organization's current facilities management programs. It emphasized the need to consistently critique and adjust your program on an ongoing basis to enhance customer service. And, it emphasized that there are at least twelve major specific areas that should be included in ongoing assessments and evaluations of facilities management programs.

## *Winning Strategies That Should be Implemented*

The major facilities management requirements in today's and tomorrow's organizations are and will continue to be that of learning and implementing the fundamentals of the profession. If people learn, understand, and can apply these fundamental strategies, they then will have a tried-and-proven base (developed on extensive industry precedents) for successfully developing and managing effective facilities management programs.

Without knowledge of these fundamental critical strategies, facilities management professionals will often be lacking what they will need to know in order to have reasonable opportunities for being successful. In other words, here are the fundamental steps that should be taken to strengthen or develop high-quality facilities management programs in today's and for tomorrow's organizations.

Determine what you want to be. Believe in its importance. Get senior leadership understanding and support. Decide what your program should include. Assess the current facilities management situation and use those findings as a basis for strengthening existing programs or developing new ones.

## Strategy 1:
### *Assess, Understand, and Document Current Programs, Policies, Processes, and Practices.*

Facilities managers (especially new facilities managers recently appointed to or just recruited for their positions) need to determine and analyze what the facilities management situation really is within their organizations. That objective can be accomplished by starting a file and carefully determining and documenting the present situations. Acquire a digital camera or a 35mm flash camera with supplies of color film and liberally take photos of existing campuses, buildings, work areas, equipment systems, furniture systems, interior layouts, and interior finishes. Focus both on the best of your organization's facilities and on the most disorganized of what you encounter. Photographically capture "the good, the bad, and the ugly!"

Build a photographic base as quickly as possible that depicts the facilities conditions as they now exist. Watch carefully for any physical areas where regulatory compliance issues may be evident. As time goes by, also take photos of work in process as improvements and changes are made. Then, as model facilities are designed, constructed, renovated, and occupied, take photos of those facilities for use as excellent examples.

Those photos will be extremely valuable as time progresses. They can be incorporated into reports to depict present situations and problems. They can be used in processes of securing program support, funding, and staffing. Ultimately, they can be included in executive briefings and staff training efforts. Photos are extremely effective, low-cost, quick-to-produce documentation of facilities management situations that exist now.

Next, start creatively gathering facts about current costs that are being endured because of the facilities management practices that exist now. Focus on those areas of current facilities management that are clearly contributing to wasted personnel time and document as much as possible where salary dollars are being wasted because of poor facilities conditions. Remember that, over time, about $9 of every $10 spent for either manufacturing or administrative work accomplishment is spent to pay the salaries, wages, and benefits of the people who do the work.

Finally, anytime someone complains about any current facilities management situation, ask them if you may jot down what they have said and if you may quote them. Gather a base of personnel reactions and client/customer reactions that can then be used to support making the facilities management improvements that are necessary. Photos, facts about current costs, and adverse reactions from personnel affected by the current facilities management situations combine to be powerful documentation when the time comes to secure approval for programs and to acquire funding, staffing, and support. Prepare yourself to present in professional but no-holds-barred ways what the real facilities management current situations and challenges really are.

This initial flurry of activity to gather photos, facts about current costs, areas where there may be regulatory compliance issues, and about client/customer reactions will result in much information coming together quickly about existing facilities management situations. Next, continue to follow through on the thorough assessments of current facilities management practices that were discussed in depth in Chapter 5 of this book. Combine all of this documentation and continue to add to it in order to have a steadily growing base of evidence about the condition of existing facilities management programs. Find, learn about, analyze, and make sure you understand what the facilities management situation really is at this point in your organization's history.

## Strategy 2:
### Secure an Executive Champion

Real-world reality is that if the owners or senior management or senior administrators decide to make something a priority, it gets structured, funded, staffed, supported and accomplished. On the other hand, if the owners or senior executives or senior administrators do not seem to care whether anything is developed or done, then it is unlikely that much will be accomplished. Strong senior management support is needed to initiate strong programs, and, ultimately, strong continuing senior management support is always needed to keep facilities management programs strong and thriving.

The entire history of organization-wide centrally-managed facilities management programs supports that programs can exist, thrive, and achieve many major benefits and returns on investment if they have ownership and senior management support. However, if there is little or only sporadic support for good facilities management programs, then it is much harder to achieve what needs to be accomplished for the overall good of organizations.

Facilities managers are encouraged to carefully assess the upper echelons of their organizations' senior management ranks and then seek out the senior leaders with whom there are existing close working relationships or where those relationships seem as though they could realistically be developed. Ask those executives if they will commit to championing facilities management programs.

## Strategy 3:
### Create a Senior-Level "Facilities Planning and Utilization Committee"

As discussed earlier in this book, individual facilities managers and their executive champions are encouraged to collaborate on the establishment of a jointly created senior-level Facilities Planning and Utilization Committee. The influence of such a committee has dramatic positive

78

impact on the level of effectiveness achieved by a facilities management program.

Strategically, the value and the power of such a committee is that it formally creates a strong connection between the strategic plans of whole organizations, which several senior members of the committee are normally involved with developing, and the facilities management organization's strategic and operating plans. The resultant integration of complementary objectives and processes creates value in many significant ways.

Financial issues are discussed and efficiently resolved. Cultural strengths are considered and this policy-setting body preserves the best of those cultural strengths. Creation and preservation of the organization's image and reputation is articulated by the senior management representatives and integrated into ongoing facilities planning, design, construction, and operation.

The representative members of a Facilities Planning and Utilization Committee are in position to consider, as they see them, the facilities requirements of their individual organizations. Other facility-related requests from all organizations are also brought to the committee for consideration. The collective requirements are assessed and as a team, resources are allocated in a way that reflects the overall objectives of the entire organization.

Often, some members of the committee and some others bringing requests to the committee do not get every one of their facilities requests completely fulfilled. But normally, everyone gets some of what they request and the resultant distribution of facilities resources provides value for each individual organization in need and respects the best interests of the organization as a whole.

This tried and proven approach improves the cycle time often needed to get facilities related projects assessed, approved, funded, and completed. An integrated approach, such as the use of a Facilities Planning and Utilization Committee, allows for broad consideration of facilities requirements and for the allocation of facilities resources that help achieve overall goals and objectives of entire organizations.

Presenting requests for facilities projects and securing support for all such initiatives is ultimately much easier and credibility is significantly enhanced for the Facilities Manager and all Facilities Management personnel when the weight and the support of a substantial committee exists. In today's fast-paced work environments, speed is important and the influence of a Facilities Planning and Utilization Committee can significantly hasten the pace for fulfillment of facilities related objectives.

## Strategy 4:
### Establish Programs That Serve Organization-Wide Facilities Management Requirements

A major objective should be the establishment of organization-wide, comprehensive, centrally-managed facilities management programs headed by individuals appropriately qualified, experienced, and motivated to be facilities managers. Virtually all organizations already have organization-wide centrally-managed accounting and finance operations headed by directors of accounting and finance.

Most organizations have similar IT (Information Technology) programs headed by Directors of IT or CIOs (Chief Information Officers). Almost all organizations have organization-wide centrally-managed human resources functions headed by Directors of Human Resources. If organizations truly want to manage their facilities as critical and valuable assets, just as the other valuable and critical assets discussed above are managed as assets, there should be formally established organization-wide centrally-managed facilities management programs headed by facilities managers. Typically, huge portions of organizations' total budgets and total worth are invested in real estate, structures, and facilities.

Facilities managers and their executive champions should develop basic facilities management program structures and policy statements, based on input from senior leaders participating in the Facilities Planning and Utilization Committee. Then these proposed facilities management structures and plans should be taken to their authorizing boards (Boards of Directors or comparable boards) to secure board approval for the establishment of organization-wide centrally-managed facilities management programs.

## Strategy 5:
### Designate a Facilities Manager

Designate (promote from within or recruit externally and hire) an appropriately qualified facilities manager. Select an individual who convinces you that she or he strongly aspires to the position and who intends to stay the course to professionally develop or strengthen and manage a comprehensive facilities management program. Select an individual with the capabilities to lead the facilities management program to a level that satisfies clients' and organizational requirements.

What qualifications should be included in the backgrounds of candidates for the position of facilities manager? Ideally, someone selected to be a facilities manager should: (1) have an appropriate academic background, preferably with a university degree or degrees in facilities management; (2) have documented work experience in facilities management; (3) have documented work experience within the industry, field, or profession for which a facility manager is being sought; (4) be a CFM—Certified Facility Manager—or someone who clearly aspires to soon become a CFM; (5) be someone whose career objective is to be a facilities manager; and (6) be an individual with the high-level personal qualities to listen, genuinely hear, assess, analyze, and take to heart the facilities management needs of organizations as expressed by the individuals who make up the occupant community.

It has been said in many professions that "most people succeeded because they were determined to succeed rather than because they were destined to succeed." Candidates who articulately, aggressively, clearly, professionally, and sincerely aspire to be professional facilities managers are needed for these extremely important positions.

# Strategy 6:
## *Determine the Best Place for Facilities Management in the Organization*

Determine the appropriate place and level in organizational structures for placement of facilities management programs. Facilities management programs should be positioned at as high a level organizationally as possible. Placement must be in a credible position within which needed funding and other resources will be made available. Many factors need to be considered when determining the most appropriate placement of facilities management programs within organizational structures. What are the existing organizational structures and hierarchies? Do centrally-managed administrative structures (for accounting, finance, IT, human resources, and others) predominate? Or, are various administrative functions widely decentralized? Have there been legal problems because of facilities-related compliance issues?

81

Remember that the potential for accomplishing what needs to be done is lessened if programs are placed at levels that are too low. Readers are encouraged to network within their own industries, fields, and professions in order to check precedents and determine how the best organizations have developed and structurally placed facilities management programs for maximum impacts and success. Remember that there is not only one answer to the question of what is the best place in an organizational structure for a facilities management program. In other words, structurally place facilities management programs where there will be maximum potential for organization-wide impact and success.

# Strategy 7:
## *Staff the Program Appropriately*

Carefully select appropriate individuals to be the staff members of facilities management programs. The people selected for facilities management positions become the next level of specialists within organizations and the liaison representatives of client/customer workgroups to facilities management programs. The ultimate success of any program is determined by selecting the most appropriate people from among those who could be available.

Provide well-developed initial and periodic orientation and training for facilities management personnel to enable their maintaining state-of-the-art professional and technical educations and expertise necessary to perform responsibilities expected of them. The success of any facilities management program will depend in large part on selecting the most appropriate personnel and in providing them with high-quality orientation, training, periodic coaching, support for continuing professional education, and effective supervision.

# Strategy 8:
## *Develop and Nurture Essential and Critical Relationships*

Facilities management programs, and facilities managers, cannot exist and work in isolation. Essential to the success of organization-wide facilities management programs will be the need to develop and nurture critical relationships of colleague leaders and professionals whose endeavors are either closely related to or are directly affected by facilities and the ways those facilities are managed. A substantial list of colleague facilities management stakeholders was identified and discussed in Chapter 4 of

82

this book. From these stakeholders come the collective knowledge, expertise, experience, precedence, and bases necessary to create high-quality totally integrated workplaces.

This strategy is so important that it is worth listing again some of the stakeholder partners that facilities managers need to enlist in totally integrated workplace design and management. Architects, audio-visual specialists, business continuity planners, civil engineers, community agency representatives, construction specialists, custodians, electrical engineers, environmental engineers, finance specialists, food services leaders, and grounds maintenance personnel all have valuable expertise to share. Information technology leaders, interior design specialists, mail services specialists, maintenance personnel, mechanical engineers, medical specialists, and procurement experts all have valuable knowledge to be tapped. Public affairs specialists, receptionists, records managers, safety engineers, security specialists, shipping and receiving leaders, supplier representatives, telecommunications specialists, tenant representatives, transportation specialists, and utilities representatives all have valuable expertise that will be needed periodically. Most of all, of course, will be the continuing support needed from senior management and management at all levels.

# Strategy 9:
## *Conduct Regularly Scheduled Executive Briefings and Staff Briefings on Facilities Management*

Periodically conduct executive briefings on facilities management issues to inform, educate, update, and continue to secure the support of organizations' senior management, management at all levels, and professional staff members. To be successful, facilities managers must keep the facilities management functions in front of the leaders of organizations. If facilities management programs slip into being well-kept secrets, then accomplishing what needs to be done is usually much more difficult than it would need to be. Executive briefings should be conducted for both internal management groups and management groups external to facilities management organizations.

Keep the executive and professional staff briefings focused, positive, upbeat, and to-the-point on agendas. Brief the leaders on what has been accomplished in facilities management and what work is underway now. Share areas where their assistance and support will be needed. Ask them for suggestions and recommendations and allow time for questions. Thank them for their participation and support. Repeat the briefings at least once every six months or as needed based on facilities management needs and operations.

Periodically conduct staff briefings on facilities management issues in order to inform, educate, update, and continue to secure the support of organizations' manufacturing, office, research, support, and other operating personnel. Use these staff briefings to identify facilities management needs, to explain work underway, and to discuss rationale for work being done.

Briefings on facilities management issues should be conducted for staff members internal to and for staff members external to facilities management departments. Keep the briefings to-the-point on agendas, positive, and upbeat. Thank attendees for their participation and support and allow time for questions. Never forget that what people have input for planning, they generally will work together to accomplish. Use the briefings to provide training, share resources, and to maintain close communications relevant to managing facilities management programs.

## Strategy 10:
### Continually Evaluate the Existing Mix of Products and Services Provided to Support Client and Organizational Requirements

The "current mix of products and services" refers to the variety and scope of the outcomes and services currently being provided by a facilities management department or unit to support client/customer needs and to meet organizational requirements. Facilities managers are reminded that those needs are continually evolving and almost constantly changing. Continually assessing your organization's current facilities management program, as discussed in Chapter 5 of this book, is essential to long-term success.

Critique, analysis, addition, deletion, modification, and updating of facilities management products and services should be done on an ongoing basis. Maintain an "open-door policy" in which personnel at all levels are encouraged to bring issues to facilities managers for discussion and consideration. Work continually and consistently with senior management, management at all levels, and personnel at all levels for purposes of responsively meeting customer/client needs and for contributing to total workplace design and management. This process is incredibly important and usually warrants the creation of a formal and structured approach that will consistently gather meaningful information to be used in the ongoing thoughtful evolution of desired facilities management products and services.

## Strategy 11:
### *Develop and Manage Workplace Standards That Support Client and Organizational Requirements*

Fundamental to the success of organization-wide facilities management programs, especially for larger organizations, is the need to develop and manage workplace standards that will support client/customer needs and organizational requirements. Space allocation, workplace equipment, office furniture, filing systems, computer resources, telecommunications, and workstation standards are among those typically established, specified, and promulgated.

For example, at the headquarters of 3M Company in St. Paul, Minnesota, during recent years, 200 square feet per administrative employee was a design benchmark used for preliminary sizing of administrative facilities. From 250 to 300 square feet per person was a standard design benchmark for preliminary sizing and planning of laboratory research facilities. While these numbers may be challenged by others, for early planning purposes within 3M they served as a valuable guide in determining how much space business units required within existing and planned facilities.

"Furniture systems" today are just that—they are truly furniture systems constructed of components that can be interconnected in widely varying configurations to meet wide varieties of workplace needs. Work surfaces, divider panels, storage compartments, filing systems, technology components, and wiring or connection devices are all acquired as components and then are assembled in varying configurations to meet varying personnel needs. Major economic advantages can thus be achieved in comparison to the purchase of non-reconfigurable components. Also, purchasing a variety of brands at low bids, for example, may not allow connectivity to existing systems. Well-coordinated facilities management planning is essential to achieve these combined objectives.

# Strategy 12:
## Select and Utilize Technology that Enhances Productivity and Responds to "Cost Containment" Programs

Facilities managers must make ongoing and concerted efforts to remain very current in their awareness and understanding of state-of-the-art technologies available for use within their organizations' work environments. Aggressive networking with colleague facilities managers in other organizations within their own industry, profession, or field will be essential in order to stay up to date about which technologies have come into wide use in organizations and environments similar to theirs. Methodically studying current IFMA and other industry literature, drawing on suppliers' expertise and resources, and periodically attending annual IFMA conventions and other relevant technology expositions should combine to form a knowledge base relative to technology implementation and use.

Examples of recent innovative technology implementation include 3M's recently patented and now widely promoted RFID (Radio Frequency Identification) technology. Small inexpensive programmable integrated circuits are essentially taped to file folders, containers of records, and other containers of many types to enable rapid location of those files and containers throughout potentially massive facilities.

Electronic access control systems are common today and reduce the need for as many security personnel as were required not all that many years ago. Computer-aided design (CAD) technologies have been in use by facilities managers for many years. Computer-assisted manufacturing (CAM) systems are common. Computer-assisted facilities management (CAFM) technologies are widely used in the day-to-day management of facilities management programs. These and other existing and evolving technologies should be used in efforts to improve productivity and to reduce costs of facilities and for operations.

# Strategy 13:
## Create Appropriate Documentation of Facilities Management Programs

Every organization can benefit in many ways from the creation and use of "facilities management websites"—or facilities management sections of organizations' websites. Today's facilities management websites should contain online: (1) complete descriptions of organization-wide facilities management program structures; (2) all facilities management policies and procedures; (3) names, phone numbers, and e-mail addresses of facilities management personnel; (4) descriptions of all categories of facilities management workplace standards; (5) an online facilities management manual; (6) online processing applications by which users can request facilities management products and services; and (7) whatever other content facilities managers and their personnel choose to make available to the personnel of their organizations.

The days of old cumbersome loose-leaf three-ring binders containing operational and procedural manuals should—as a rule of thumb—now be things of the past. In years gone by, many facilities management and other organizational programs often wasted enormous sums of money to produce multiple copies of paper manuals, only to have them end up on shelves and rarely being updated and often not being used. Today's facilities management websites with a myriad of facilities management resources maintained online makes each and every document or part of the content "living documents" that can readily be updated, eliminated, or replaced. Make a major goal of developing state-of-the-art and current-to-the-moment documentation supporting organization-wide facilities management programs.

## Strategy 14:
### Join and Participate in Professional Associations That Provide Ongoing Training, Publications, and Resources for Facilities Managers

There are professional associations related to almost every occupation and facilities management is no exception. Professional associations are great sources of industry-related information that can often be accessed through networking with members, reading industry news articles and publications, catalogs provided by suppliers, trade shows and conventions, magazines, research reports, and other resources. Workers should seek out and join a professional association related to their field of work.

As a reminder from Chapter 1 of this book, IFMA, the International Facility Management Association, was founded in 1980, The association currently has about 17,500 members in 125 chapters spanning over 50 countries. In addition to others, the IFMA provides all the resources referenced in the preceding paragraph. Everyone working in the facilities management or a related profession should consider joining IFMA. The IFMA, including it's mailing address, phone number, and web-site address, is listed as a facilities management resource in Chapter 15 of this book.

Other professional associations with goals, objectives, and members either directly related or closely related to the work of facilities managers includes the AIA, ANSI, ARSEG, ASID, ASTM, BIFM, BIFMA, BOMA, EPA, FMAA, FMN, GSA, IBD, IBI, IDRC, IIDA, IREM, ISO, JFMA, NACORE, NCIDQ, NIOSH, NOPA, and OSHA. Descriptions of all of these excellent organizations and the resources available through them are beyond the scope of this short book. Readers are encouraged to seek out their web-sites and to become familiar with the resources available through these individual and collective high-quality organizations. See the IFMA website to access information about each of these colleague professional associations and organizations.

# Strategy 15:
## *Become a Certified Facility Manager*

One of the most meaningful ways for individuals to become acknowledged as competent professionals is to earn certification in their chosen professions. Along with many other professional associations, the IFMA, in addition to many other services, offers and maintains a certification program. The IFMA Certified Facility Manager (CFM) program is designed to assess competency earned through work experience, education, and understanding that is demonstrated by successfully passing a rigorous exam. Not easy to earn, the CFM credential adds prestige and credibility to the level of competence achieved by individuals.

Perhaps more important than earning the CFM designation, is the knowledge and skills that facilities management personnel must accumulate in order to pass the CFM exam. With or without the CFM designation, knowledge of facilities management principles is critical to the success or failure of any practicing professional. While one should certainly strive to earn the CFM credential, there is even greater value in accumulating and applying the knowledge and skills that one needs to become a successful facilities management professional. Preparation for the CFM exam will help one accumulate that knowledge. Passing the exam and earning the CFM credential is "frosting on the cake."

Of the approximately 17,500 members of the IFMA, about 3,500 currently have earned the CFM credential. That statistic in itself tells us that

CFMs are members of a prestigious group. For information about becoming a Certified Facility Manager, go to the IFMA website at www.ifma.com.

## *Summary*

The "winning strategies for high-quality facilities management" presented in this chapter have evolved to become the steps that should be taken in most organizations to either strengthen or develop organization-wide facilities management programs that will have a high probability of being successful. The authors assume that readers, facilities managers, and others responsible for facilities management will methodically assess their organization's current facilities management situations to determine the structure, advantages, disadvantages, costs, and impacts on people of programs now in place. Implement the 15 winning strategies discussed in this chapter to strengthen or develop YOUR organization-wide facilities management program.

# Chapter 7
## OFFICE LAYOUT AND DESIGN: EXPERIENCED INSIGHTS

### Total Facilities Planning and the Development of Productive Offices and Interiors

Offices are essential in small businesses, major corporations, government agencies at all levels, not-for-profit entities, professional practices, schools, churches, and in organizations of all types. Growing numbers of offices also exist within homes. We now live in a world economy that is an information society in which millions of employed persons work in or from an office base.

Offices and other settings are places where decisions are made. Few individuals want to make the key decisions in their lives; whether or not to marry, whether or not to have children, which career to select, which home to purchase; without an adequate base of information related to those decisions. And, very few people want to make those key personal and family decisions simply by flipping a coin. They want relevant, complete, accurate and current-to-the-moment information as a basis for making those decisions. Offices and other settings are repositories of information needed to make well-informed decisions.

Corporate and other leaders would be equally foolish to make key strategic or operating decisions by flipping coins. Heads or tails, do we purchase that company or do we not? Heads or tails, do we perform surgery or do we not? Heads or tails, do we hire those people and add those new product lines or do we not? Such approaches to decision making would be foolhardy and would obviously result in many incorrect choices and expensive disasters.

Reality is that, whether in an office or an operating room, whenever decisions are made without ready access to relevant, complete, accurate, and current-to-the moment information, the often-resulting decision by guessing or by chance can result in very bad outcomes. Great information and records are phenomenally important critical resources for making appropriate decisions regularly and consistently. And, information and records are major products (outputs) of work performed within offices.

We have come a long way from the offices of 60 years ago where workplace equipment and technology consisted primarily of desks, chairs, typewriters, telephones, mechanical calculators, drawer filing cabinets, spirit or stencil duplicators, and possibly a telegraph or a teletype. Even the most creative office designs of the World War II era were often desks arranged in straight rows with personnel feverishly working in assembly-line arrangements.

One change that has not happened as quickly as many predicted years ago is the reality that the paperless office has not yet arrived and business and government still rely heavily on paper document records. We live in an age when so much work can be accomplished via computers and digital information. Yet it is interesting and somewhat saddening to note that two of the most commonly used technologies for managing recorded information in today's offices continue to be old drawer file cabinets and 12 inch by 15 inch cardboard boxes.

State-of-the-art facilities should provide the physical settings within which information is managed and work is accomplished. Effective office facilities should be developed to be control, communications, processing, and administrative nerve centers operating at peak efficiency thus enabling organizations to prosper, compete, and succeed. And, office environments have strong and direct effects on the quality and quantity of work produced in offices as well as on the morale of all inhabitants within facilities.

The professional field of study known as ergonomics has evolved to address challenges such as worker productivity, morale, and related issues. As a field of study, ergonomics investigates how the performance and morale of workers on the job are dependent on the physiological and psychological factors in personnel work environments. Ergonomics integrates the use of space, technologies, furniture, and the physiological factors of light, color, sound, and temperature to meet psychological needs of personnel inhabiting workplaces.

Large investments are made in personnel, buildings, facilities, technologies, equipment, systems, supplies, and related support functions. However, offices in many organizations have more or less simply evolved to their present state without the benefit of systematic planning and management. Managerially, much more needs to be done in so many places.

Office and workplace design is influenced by merging, upsizing, downsizing, and rightsizing — all strategies being widely implemented and then explained and analyzed in the world's news media. Running lean and mean is now much more common than going fat and slow. Many organizations are changing to flattened hierarchical structures with a thinning of middle-management ranks coming along with cuts in staff sizes. More extensive use of matrix and team structuring is taking place in order to accomplish major projects, objectives, and goals. And the people of organizations are expected to adapt and must adapt if they are to be employed, competitive, and successful.

Office space is a valuable economic resource that often fluctuates in terms of availability, supply, and cost. In business centers within most city environments, there are times when searches for more space for growing workforces lead to increased demands and higher prices for space. At other times, vacancy rates of 30 to 40 percent or more are not uncommon.

Office space and how it is configured and conditioned directly impacts on the personnel who inhabit and use that space. The management of office space, like the management of other economic resources, is an ongoing process that requires continual attention for purposes of gleaning the most value possible for each space dollar spent. Facilities managers routinely face ten major office layout and design challenges of:

➡ Making or participating in decisions to determine appropriate geographic office locations;

➡ Providing office space that is needed through renovating or modifying existing space, purchasing or leasing existing facilities, or planning and constructing new buildings;

➡ Juggling the year-to-year costs for space during dynamic times in which there may be rapid expansion or contraction in needs for space;

➡ Coordinating the work of architects, designers, systems analysts, industrial engineers, unit heads, industrial psychologists, human resources personnel, records managers, IT professionals, and other stakeholders to accomplish ergonomically-engineered total workplace design and management;

➡ Interacting with users at all levels and with management to create office layouts designed around the work to be accomplished;

➡ Making the best use of office space in ways that will enable inhabitants' work to be done both easier and faster;

➡ Meeting personnel comfort needs while improving and maintaining attractive office appearances;

➡ Adjusting the designs, manipulation of physical environments, and utilization of ergonomic elements that will nurture climates for increased productivity and enhance the individual and collective inhabitant morale;

➡ Continually assessing the adequacy of office locations, physical environments, and arrangement of physical components within available space to provide maximum effectiveness;

➡ Providing as much flexibility as realistically possible for future expansion, contraction, and change.

Facilities managers find that their work is especially critical and important whenever new office buildings are being planned, when existing buildings need to be renovated, or whenever existing offices are being analyzed with objectives of strategically grouping people, technology, furniture, equipment, and their surroundings more effectively. Facilities managers need to work toward the major goal of creating well-planned layouts in which there can be an efficient, timely, and economical flow of information to those persons responsible for decision making at various levels within organizations.

## What Usually Triggers Changes in Office Space Needs?

Office space needs and utilization changes are usually triggered by one or a combination of: (1) establishment of a new entity, business, division, agency, branch, department, or unit; (2) increases or downsizing of organizations, work, or personnel; (3) changes in organizational structures; (4) changes in technology utilization; or (5) personnel reactions to the adequacy of their facilities and surroundings. New office buildings and areas usually permit coordinated space planning. Renovation of existing buildings or areas usually poses more difficult-to-solve problems. As a result, providing office space and accomplishing high-quality office layout and design planning can be both fascinating and frustrating.

# Where Should Offices Be Located?

Offices may be located in various places including office parks, specialty-professional office buildings, office condominiums, and self-contained urban complexes. The unique situations and needs of individual organizations should be the major factors when considering office locations. Some organizations will consider new buildings only, some prefer to focus on modernizing older buildings, some select major metropolitan areas, while others opt for more rural settings.

Factors to be considered when determining office locations include—but certainly are not limited to—proximity to important business factors such as customers or clients, quality and condition of surrounding geographic areas, and the stability of other tenants in shared buildings. Other factors to be considered include the availability of buildings or potential buildings, costs of those facilities, characteristics of the buildings, adaptability of the space, existing lighting and ventilation and related environmental factors, building security, and freedom from noise or other distractions. Aggressive networking by facilities managers for purposes of knowing and understanding what decisions their organizations' competitors have made and are making relative to office location decisions will be important to their long-term success.

# Owning or Leasing Space?

There is some level of prestige associated with owning facilities. Ownership of facilities permits buildings to be custom-designed and constructed for the unique and particular needs of organizations. In planning new owned buildings, generally the essential physical features such as number of floors, support rooms for technology, records storage and management rooms, supporting pillars, stairs, elevators, escalators, cafeterias, and other amenities can be planned and located where they are most desirable.

When moving into existing buildings that are purchased and where the physical features were planned by former owners or tenants, then planning and arrangement of work areas often requires working around fixed factors. In owned facilities, modifications and changes can also be made as organizational needs change. Publicity value of organizational names visibly placed on owned buildings can be high, and ownership has historically been a relatively safe investment.

Major advantages of leasing include retention of financial flexibility without having large amounts of capital tied up in relatively long-term building investments. If the ongoing space requirements of an organization are very likely to change rapidly over the next few years, then—generally—strong consideration should be given to leasing. Leasing does not tie organizations down to owned locations, frees lessees from some responsibilities and worries of ownership, and avoids many building maintenance and repair concerns. Is it better to own or to lease? As with many business decisions, there are advantages and disadvantages to both choices.

## Analyzing and Determining Office Space Needs

The organization of a corporation, company, firm, government agency, or other type of entity always directly affects the layouts of manufacturing plants, distribution facilities, and offices. In many large corporations such as manufacturing firms, the production and office facilities are frequently separated. Many organizations of these types also have branch or warehouse offices that are decentralized geographically.

In service organizations such as insurance companies and banks, direct customer service and information are the major products, and offices are the major facilities that are needed. Before many important building and facilities development decisions can be made relative to office space needs, a thorough analysis should be undertaken to gather current and relevant information.

Here again, facilities managers are strongly encouraged to network with other facilities managers in order to learn and understand how to most effectively conduct appropriate office space needs analyses. Information that should be gathered and that will be very relevant to planning office buildings and office space includes:

- Business, entity, division, department, or work group name;

- The organization's official description of the business, division, department, or work groups that are to be housed in planned space or that occupies existing buildings and space being analyzed;

- An operations manual, strategic plan, or similar documentation that explains the major functions of the business, division, department, or work groups that are to be housed in planned space;

- An organization chart or charts for the function or functions that are to be housed in planned space;

- An explanation of the other entities, divisions, departments, or work groups from which information is received as well as those entities, divisions, departments, or work groups to which the planned office or offices being analyzed transmit information;

- Amount and type of contact with internal personnel from other units of the organization;

- Amount and type of contact with the public (customers, clients, patients, students, citizens, constituents);

- Relationship of the entity, division, department, or work group with other entities, divisions, departments, or work groups. In other words, which other entities are in frequent or regular communication with an entity under study and what is the nature of those communications;

- Number of personnel that will inhabit the planned space or inhabit the space being analyzed;

- Functions of personnel in each job or position category;

- Types of space necessary to meet unique requirements of each person in the entity, division, department, or work group;

- Changes expected in numbers of personnel and in the activities and functions of the organization;

- Information technology (computers, servers, printers, scanners, copiers, fax units, phones, or other technologies) and other specialized equipment presently in use by personnel or expected to be used by personnel;

- Records stored and managed, types of media stored and managed, current volumes of records stored and managed, volumes of records expected in the future, retention schedules that exist covering those records, and a summary of records management issues presented by the personnel;

- Explanation of special workplaces (reception areas, conference rooms, private offices) that will be needed in space being planned or in office space currently being analyzed; and

➡ Other information deemed to be relevant based on experience in space planning (office layout and design) functions within your own industry or field.

A thorough process of gathering and compiling the above information should then enable identification of the following space needs: (1) working space for personnel required by each individual assigned to the entity, division, department, or work group; (2) support space required for services such as records management, reception areas, copying and mail centers, and conference rooms; and (3) traffic-flow space such as elevators, escalators, lobbies, corridors, and aisles used by customers, clients, internal personnel, and the general public.

It usually is not difficult to collect information on the present space occupied by an organization, but it is more complex to accurately determine work relationships among entities and between and among people. Again, remember the extremely important principle that when designing or redesigning any facility, facilities should be built and designed around the work to be done—good ways of doing work should not have to be changed to meet the constraints of inflexible facilities.

## Answer the PEOPLE, INFORMATION, PROCESS, TECHNOLOGY, and PLACE Questions

Co-author Mark Langemo has been teaching office planning, layout, and design fundamentals within university business school settings for many years. He has consulted, conducted in-organization training, and presented management seminars to practitioners for many years. While it may seem an oversimplification of what can be and often are more involved processes, there is practical merit for facilities managers to boil down the analysis process to that of securing answers to four key groups of questions—the people questions, the process questions, the technology questions, and the space questions.

The key people questions to be asked and answered with supporting information gathered as a basis for thorough office space planning, layout, and design are:

➡ WHO ARE THE PEOPLE who work here now?

➡ WHAT DO EACH OF THEM DO—what are their responsibilities and tasks?

➡ WHERE DO THEY DO THEIR WORK now?

➡ WHAT DO THEY NEED TO WORK WITH in order to do their work?

➡ HOW DO THEY COMMUNICATE AND WITH WHOM while they are working?

➡ HOW DO THEY FEEL ABOUT THEIR SITUATION at work now?

The key information questions to be asked and answered are:

➡ WHO CREATES THE INFORMATION required by the organization?

➡ WHAT INFORMATION IS CREATED in the course of business?

➡ WHY IS THE INFORMATION CREATED and used?

➡ WHO USES THE INFORMATION in the performance of work?

➡ HOW IS THE INFORMATION USED within the organization?

➡ WITH WHOM IS THE INFORMATION EXCHANGED AND SHARED within and outside the organization?

➡ HOW LONG IS THE INFORMATION RETAINED with respect to records retention requirements?

➡ WHAT MEDIA IS USED TO STORE THE INFORMATION for effective and efficient use?

➡ WHERE IS THE INFORMATION STORED and protected?

The key process questions to be asked and answered are:

➡ WHAT ARE THE HIGH-VOLUME TYPES OF WORK done in this entity (unit)?

➡ WHO RECEIVES OR INITIATES the information and/or work?

➡ WHERE DOES WORK MOVE/FLOW from its start to completion?

➡ WHAT HAPPENS AT EACH STEP in the process now?

➡ WHERE DOES WORK END UP—transmitted, filed digitally or on paper, deleted?

The key technology questions to be asked and answered are:

➡ WHAT TECHNOLOGIES AND EQUIPMENT are in use now?

➡ WHO USES WHAT TECHNOLOGIES AND EQUIPMENT now?

➡ WHAT PURPOSES DOES THE TECHNOLOGY OR EQUIPMENT serve?

➡ WHERE IS TECHNOLOGY PHYSICALLY PLACED now?

The key place questions to be asked and answered are:

➡ WHAT IS THE SIZE AND SHAPE OF THE SPACE IN USE NOW?

➡ WHAT IS THE LIGHTING situation throughout the space now?

➡ WHAT ARE THE COLORS in use throughout the surroundings now?

➡ WHAT ARE THE CONDITIONS OF THE AIR throughout the space now?

➡ WHAT IS THE SIZE & SHAPE OF THE SPACE THAT COULD BE AVAILABLE?

Facilities managers who have gathered and summarized information discussed above can, as a result, consider personnel space needs, special workplaces, storage areas, and interpersonal and inter-organizational communication needs as reported relative to planned space or existing space under analysis. From the square feet estimated, facilities managers can consult their organization's established space guidelines, or use generic guidelines available from the IFMA and other resources, to determine how much space should be allocated in space planning for the entire entity and for each workplace and inhabitant. Fixed percentages of aisle space can be added to determine the total square feet needed for the entity, division, agency, department, or work group.

## Major Elements to be Considered in Planning Productive Offices

The key elements for facilities managers, office designers, and others to consider when planning new office buildings, planning new office space, or when renovating existing office space include:

➡ Work flow;

➡ Communication patterns;

100

- Individual personnel space requirements;

- Office traffic;

- Technology and equipment requirements;

- Flexibility and expansion;

- Elimination of hazards;

- Space available or that could be made available;

- Budget limitations; and

- Individual and collective personnel preferences.

## *What Really Are Human Space Needs?*

The experiences of veteran facilities managers backed up by results of formal research collectively support that because of unique personality and cultural features of office personnel, there needs to be thoughtful consideration given to certain human needs when planning offices. Most important, each individual needs a certain amount of personal space—an area of privacy surrounding individuals that is important for minimizing distractions. The amount of personal space desired and beneficial for psychological comfort differs between introverts and extroverts and also varies widely for people from different cultures. Research time should be devoted to carefully considering the makeup of any workgroup being analyzed for purposes of planning appropriate amounts of personal space.

Quite closely related to personal space is the concept of territoriality which refers to the physical area that is under the control of workers and designed and designated for their use. In offices, territoriality is commonly defined as the workplaces assigned to individual workers. Territoriality also commonly implies status, power, and authority. Since so much work in offices requires interaction of people, it is very important to understand that workplace arrangements affect interpersonal communications.

The needs of disabled individuals must also be carefully considered and planned for very thoughtfully and carefully. Typical of workplace requirements for the disabled are door widths that accommodate wheelchairs; handrails; ramps; lowered water fountains and lavatories; and elevator controls with Braille symbols next to floor buttons and placed low enough to be reached from a wheelchair.

# Major Trends in Office Facilities Development

Exciting major trends in office facilities development include: (1) increasingly intelligent buildings interconnected with fiber-optic and other cabling to link and integrate information systems technologies; (2) continuing refinements in ergonomically-engineered workplaces equipped with relevant technologies so that human anatomy, physiology, and psychology considerations will permeate workplace development; and (3) refinement of open-plan office environments. Offices equipped with modular interior systems are designed to facilitate interpersonal and interpersonnel communications, enable efficient workflow, maximize technology applications, foster esprit-de-corps, and provide the greatest amount of effective facilities at the lowest practical costs.

Forward-thinking facilities management professionals are contributing to high-quality information resource management within organizations through working closely with colleague leaders in IT, records management, administrative services, and others to identify information needs, workflow requirements, management and personnel workplace requirements, and related human factors essential for success. Then, they are incorporating the best of architectural, engineering, space planning, environmental, interior design, and human factors principles and precedence to develop and manage state-of-the-art offices and complete facilities.

## Alternative Office Design Plans

Traditional conventional-plan office layout and design arrangements are the older and more familiar approach to office facilities development. Conventional-plan offices are often quite high-density regimented row-by-row layouts coupled with many traditional private offices in which symmetry and uniformity are decisive considerations. A neat and orderly appearance is usually initially achieved, and personnel are placed in comfortable areas typically reflecting their relative position in organizational hierarchies. The emphasis is heavily upon tradition, work, efficiency, and cost. A negative factor is that arguably 20 to 40 percent of office space is often wasted in conventional-plan offices.

Characteristics of conventional-plan offices include wall barriers that tend to isolate work areas. Critics of this plan believe that it reduces and minimizes human interaction and also tends to hinder interdepartmental workflow. Conventional office layout plans generally lead to more inflexible arrangements and often add to the cost of redesigning offices. To be used effectively, conventional office layout and design plans should be very carefully developed. Organizations should be arranged so that the work-flow proceeds in uninterrupted manners and passes through as few hands as possible.

Planning of conventional-plan offices should be done only after careful study of administrative systems and procedures, identification of technology applications and use, arrangement of workstations and furniture and technology, and after consideration of the requirements and preferences of personnel. Units or departments with considerable public contact should generally be located near entrances and have direct access to hallways in order to minimize traffic flow.

In contrast, flexible-personnel office layout and design approaches or open-plan workstations, sometimes referred to as office landscaping, emphasize the avoidance of sameness throughout layouts. Priorities are given to open planning which stresses consideration for workflows, traffic patterns, and communication networks and a minimizing of privacy and privilege. Open planning tends to feature large open landscapes rather than enclosed or separated areas. Panels and dividers of varying heights replace many partitions. Modular workstations, furniture and technology placed in functional clusters, and irregularly arranged workstations are common features.

Open-plan office layout and design approaches have become extremely popular because they bring together the functional, behavioral, and technical factors needed to design workplaces for work groups as well as for individuals and departments or units. It is now estimated that about 75 percent of white-collar personnel inhabit and work in open-plan offices. Open-plan features include space that is free of permanent walls and corridors. Workstations are arranged by using movable elements such as desks, chairs, freestanding panels, media shelves, files, and live plants without changing the fixed installations (light fixtures, heating and air-conditioning outlets, partitions, or floor coverings).

In open plans, each individual grouping of workstations is usually arranged without regard for windows or other traditional design limitations and in non-uniform fashions dictated by natural lines of information flow and human communications needs. In theory, open-plan offices do not include private offices but instead with privacy provided by using plants and movable sound-absorbing panels or partitions that are wired for communications and technology connections. The status of personnel is determined more by their work assignments than by their locations. Higher-level executives may have larger amounts of space and larger desks but with few other visible signs of rank.

In real-world practice, however, open-plan offices are often combined with more conventional plans so that high-level executives, administrators, and leaders can be accommodated in private offices for more isolation and confidentiality. Management must ultimately weigh the relative advantages and disadvantages of using private offices. Private offices often create prestige in the eyes of visitors for top management, senior leaders, and higher-level staff personnel.

Often, some tenants and other people believe that the confidential nature of work performed by senior leaders such as planning, research, financial planning, human resources planning, and related work requires more privacy and higher levels of concentration than other functions. The use of private offices is more expensive in terms of providing utilities such as lighting, heating, and air conditioning. Private offices are somewhat inflexible because their relatively permanent partitions are expensive and difficult to move or remove. And sometimes, private offices create arbitrary barriers to interpersonal and interpersonnel communications.

In summary, advantages of open-plan office layout and design approaches include: (1) the ability to design and build offices around the work to be done, (2) lower construction costs, (3) reduced energy costs, (4) more usable office space—which may run as high as 80-90 percent of available space, and (5) flexibility of arrangements. Disadvantages of open-plan approaches include: (1) limitations on privacy, (2) too many distractions, (3) too much noise, and (4) sometimes hastily or poorly designed office layouts.

## *Workplaces for People in Offices*

Offices, as we know them, are thinking places and workplaces for personnel. Individuals need to be placed in locations and situations appropriate for thinking, for managing information, communicating, exchanging and distributing information, and for performing essential work. The most basic unit of office space is individual workstations where personnel perform the bulk of their assigned work. These workstations in combination become group work centers for many personnel to collectively work together.

As stated earlier, office layout and design planning should be based on analyses of work to be performed, communication requirements, technology requirements, information storage and retrieval requirements, and unique related needs. No one workstation exists by or for itself but must serve as part of larger groups accommodating people that are working toward common goals. Work centers, as a result, must be space planned and coordinated to fit into total workplace environments.

## Tools and Systems for Use in Office Space Planning

Architects, interior designers, professional office space planners, facilities managers, and others concerned about high-quality office layout and design have evolved several tools and systems for use in accomplishing their work. Most basic of those tools are plastic templates which are readily available from office systems and furniture suppliers. Cutout areas within these templates indicate common sizes and shapes of various types of furniture, filing cabinets, columns, and partitions.

Another traditional and basic approach is the use of colored paper cutouts of all types of furniture, equipment, partitions, columns, and dividers prepared to the same scale (1/8" or 1/4") for planning appropriate locations and relationships. Simulated office space models using replicas of selected office areas are sometimes prepared by architectural, interior design, and office planning professionals.

Most common today, of course, is the use of computer-aided design (CAD) technologies for automation of planning and drafting functions. CAD is made possible through computer programming techniques that have resulted in off-the-shelf software available for quickly doing the line drawing and insertion of various geometric shapes necessary to develop office layout designs. CAD is used for many functions in addition to office layout and design—such as for designing items in engineering settings, for mapping and plotting, and for a wide variety of computer-augmented development functions.

## The Potential of Intelligent Buildings

Today, office designers must consider the potential for intelligent buildings that are constructed to include computer-based technologies and appropriate communications connections containing sensors that enable monitoring and interacting with building conditions. Building maintenance personnel and other occupants are able to access and monitor building management systems consisting of security control, fire control, energy management, environmental and lighting controls, and elevator and escalator controls. Shared occupant services are typically available for voice communications, computer networks, data transmission, and wide varieties of administrative services.

Many shared building owners (landlords) now lease space to occupants ranging from individual offices to major organizations. There continues to be a steadily emerging market for intelligent building space available for lease in which potential lessees can have access to and can connect to current-to-the-moment technologies. Leasing frees those occupants from the financial and planning responsibilities necessary for providing their own buildings, space, maintenance, and other related services.

## More About Ergonomics

Personnel in office workplaces, if they are to be productive, must be housed in physical settings that are well planned and that incorporate the best conditions for meeting their work requirements and personal needs. Such settings include surface environments made attractive and pleasant through appropriate uses of color and texture. Environments for seeing require adequate amounts of light and high levels of visual comfort.

Good hearing environments involve managing noise by providing music or other pleasant background sounds that tend to stimulate toward productivity. Comfortable air environments are necessary with controls maintained through sophisticated heating, ventilation, and air conditioning systems. Security is essential for both the physical safety and the mental well being of all personnel located in total workplace environments.

Specific issues related to ergonomics, and ergonomics issues important to facilities managers, are discussed in other portions of this book. Understanding how all of these environmental factors combine for contribution to productive offices and other workplaces is essential for the success of professional facilities managers.

## Summary

Professional facilities managers are usually responsible for providing well-planned workplace environments that will contribute to successful, productive, and timely accomplishment of work by those people responsible for performing that work. In developing these workplaces, facilities managers must be concerned about meeting space needs and personnel needs so that these workplaces facilitate workflow as well as the formal and informal communications requirements of all inhabitants. Effective building development and utilization of space must be carefully planned based on thorough analyses of organizational needs, goals, and objectives.

# Chapter 8

## ROLES OF FACILITIES MANAGEMENT IN HEALTH, SAFETY, AND ENVIRONMENT

### *Facilities Managers Should be Integrators and Facilitators Who Make Health, Safety, and Environmental Issues High Priorities*

Facilities managers fill roles similar to that of "landlords" who own and lease rental homes, apartment buildings, resort living accommodations, townhome complexes, or inner-city luxury loft residences. Other landlords own and lease commercial properties including individual executive and professional offices, office suites, office suites with shared tenant services, whole floor work areas, entire buildings, or campuses combining offices with factories and warehouses and related workplaces.

Landlords—especially those owners of high-quality properties who endeavor to be professional, progressive, caring, tenant-sensitive landlords in the truest sense of the word—usually do many important things. The best of them are accessible and dependable "go-to landlords" who make themselves readily and consistently available when tenant needs of all kinds occur. Those needs commonly include space or changing requirements for space; maintenance of structures; and maintenance of heating, cooling, electrical, and other systems. Landlords typically assure that facilities are designed, constructed, and operated in safe, healthy, secure, and efficient ways.

Landlords are routinely called on when even minor upset conditions occur—when hail pounds roofs, when windstorms cause havoc, when tides wash away landscaping, when interruptions to electrical supplies happen, or when sewers overflow. Landlords usually need to be first on the scenes when major events take place such as fires, explosions, serious storm damage, or attacks by terrorists. Landlords typically are involved with events on a spectrum from trivial (coffee being spilled on carpeting) to catastrophic (terrorists flying airliners into major skyscrapers).

## Facilities Managers Function as Landlords
## Landlords Function as Facilities Managers

Facilities managers are often viewed as landlords within organizations in that they are usually at the very center of virtually all facilities-related situations that occur. The CEO says "we need more space—call Facilities Management." A custodian says "the new carpet cleaning solution doesn't take the stains out of visitor-area carpets—call Facilities Management." A receptionist upset that an area of a building still is not smoke free says— "call Facilities Management." A manufacturing supervisor needs more room to turn and unload large trucks and says—"call Facilities Management." And the No. 1 facilities complaint in the workplace is "it's too cold/hot in here—call Facilities Management."

The value of professional facilities management expertise is really magnified when senior management strategic planning results in decisions like 3M Company's decision in the early 1980s to build a new office and lab complex in Austin, Texas. Almost instantly, major facilities decisions needed to emerge one after the other after the other until that complex was created and occupied. Earlier in this book, it was stressed that today's and tomorrow's professional facilities managers should be integral parts of organizations' senior management groups. Facilities managers often need to be involved in the largest and most expensive ventures undertaken within entire organizations.

Facilities managers—during exciting times of major expansion as well as during more calm and routine times—must be proactive leaders in working to assure that health, safety, and environmental issues remain high priorities. Health, safety, and environmental features must always be factored into facilities design, construction, renovation, occupancy, and use.

## 3M Example Relative to Environmental Issues

At 3M, part of the corporate culture had been that senior executives were always unanimous in their determination and commitment to assure that health, safety, and environmental issues were major considerations in the ongoing management of this highly-successful research, new product development, manufacturing, and marketing company. Senior management's collective position was always that corporate personnel should consistently strive to do it right when it comes to all health, safety, and environmental issues that are associated with the endeavors of 3M.

One example is 3M's 3P (Pollution-Prevention-Pays) program introduced in the early 1970s which put into more aggressive practice a corporate philosophy that pollution should be eliminated at its source and that if pollution is eliminated before it is created then many potential environmental problems will never become real problems. Elimination of any and every pollution at its source was also stressed because elimination of pollution at its potential sources often saves money.

Renowned for their proactive pollution prevention strategies, the leadership and personnel of 3M earned considerable good publicity that culminated in an enhanced and well earned corporate reputation as an environmentally-sensitive company. The immediate and long-term value of these practices are that the environment is protected and, while doing so, the company also reduced costs and minimized vulnerability to compliance and other potentially adverse consequences. 3M continues to practice the principles of the 3P Program to this day.

3M continues to benefit from life-cycle pollution prevention. Life-cycle pollution prevention involves using environmentally friendly raw materials at the front end of product manufacturing cycles while also considering the longer-term usability and eventual disposal characteristics of products. Manufacturing workers and other occupants of 3M facilities and consumers of 3M products are consequently more broadly protected from potentially harmful substances. And, potentially harmful substances are not discharged into the environment.

Many 3M products are used in the design, construction, furnishings, equipment, and finishes of a myriad of facilities constructed and occupied by 3M personnel. And, many 3M products are used in the design, manufacture, and construction of thousands of other products produced by other companies worldwide. For many years, a formal senior-level 3M Health, Safety, and Environment Committee operated under the direction of the CEO and the Corporate Operations Committee. Executives appointed to this committee were responsible for making sure that all health, safety, and environmental issues were addressed and managed.

## 3M Example Relative to Health Concerns

3M's Medical Department worked very closely with Facilities Management and with research and manufacturing leadership. They worked to assure that industrial hygienists and toxicologists were involved with the selection of raw materials, and they developed procedures for handling raw materials associated with research, development, and manufacturing of products. Their intent was to ensure that 3M personnel and consumers of the company's products would not be dangerously exposed to harmful materials.

The 3M Medical Department also worked with Facilities Management to assure that emergency squads were established and equipped in order to provide emergency responses to employee and visitor injuries, illnesses, or other health problems. Emergency squads were established in each building. If an employee or visitor, for example, experienced a heart attack, the emergency squads would respond to the incident and on their way to the incident would go to sites within buildings where defibrillators and other medical supplies were available and take those materials with them to the scene of the incident. Facilities Management funded the purchase of defibrillators and other medical supplies to equip selected sites throughout the entire 3M headquarters complex.

Other examples where Facilities Management and the 3M Medical Department worked together included routine and continuous monitoring and testing the quality of drinking water and air supplies. Testing for mold, spores, bacteria, and other unwanted substances was routinely conducted in HVAC ductwork, carpeting, rest rooms, and general workplace environments. Other health-related situations on which Facilities Management and 3M's Medical department teamed up were to monitor long-term personnel exposure to company work environments, especially in laboratory and manufacturing environments. 3M's long-term management of health, safety, and environmental issues means that 3M personnel, consumers, and the environment combine to be long-term winners.

## 3M Example Relative to Safety

Facilities Management and the Corporate Safety Department worked together to assure that safety teams were established and existed in all 3M facilities. Safety teams were responsible for performing routine and regularly scheduled inspections to identify and remedy potential safety hazards. If structural modifications were required to assure compliance with safety regulations or building codes, Facilities Management would take steps to accomplish those modifications. Facilities Management personnel were also trained and familiar with building and safety codes that were required to be integrated into facilities design, construction, renovation, and operations.

Regulations related to confined space entry and electrical lockout/tagout are among many health, safety, and environmental regulations designed to protect the welfare of maintenance workers. Facilities Management, Corporate Safety, and medical departments often work together to enable compliance with such safety regulations and to minimize the possibility of maintenance workers being harmed or injured while doing their work.

"Confined space" refers to compact areas such as tanks, storage bins, hoppers, vaults, pits, sewers, manholes, or any other space with limited openings for entry or exit, unfavorable natural ventilation, or not designed for continuous occupancy but occasionally containing electrical, plumbing, air handling, or other specialized equipment or systems that require some kind of periodic repair or adjustment and requires people to enter such spaces to perform service work. There are OSHA regulations that restrict workers from entering such environments without other personnel being present in the immediate area.

The co-authors of this book were young men during the Vietnam War, and Dan Brathal is a veteran of that conflict. Whenever the term "confined space" surfaces in facilities management work, it brings back memories of our U. S. Army and Marine "tunnel rats" from that conflict. These troops faced the challenges of crawling into small dark tunnels—the hideouts of enemy troops—armed with flashlights and .38 snubnose revolvers only to encounter booby traps, snakes, or armed enemy. Readers are asked to imagine the claustrophobia and sheer terror that many armed forces personnel faced as tunnel rats serving our country with their courage. Going into confined space by yourself without anyone nearby for support then and now can be hazardous to your health.

"Lockout/tagout" refers to circumstances in which maintenance workers or others may be working on electrical systems. OSHA regulations require that advance notification be provided so that electrical supplies in the vicinity of or for the item to directly be worked upon be shut off and "tagged" to indicate that power supplies have been certifiably shut off (locked out). The lockout/shutoff must be verified through use of bright-colored highly-visible tags (tagout) so workers will know and be assured that power supplies have been shut off and that systems are safe. Facilities managers and safety managers should work together to make sure that these procedures are developed and are implemented regularly and consistently in day-to-day practice.

Lockout/tagout regulations and confined space entry regulations are simply two of many types of regulations that influence facilities maintenance and repair activities. Since human safety is paramount in facilities management operations, such regulations must be carefully and consistently implemented.

## Health, Safety, and Environmental Impacts on Facilities Managers

Facilities managers are often charged with responsibilities for identification, interpretation, translation, and implementation of numerous codes and regulations related to health, safety, and environmental issues. Often it is the responsibility of facilities management professionals to post in visible locations notices that describe and explain such regulations for the ultimate benefit of all personnel within workplaces. In many instances, laws require that such postings be made and—in increasing numbers of situations—that specific formalized personnel training be provided relative to health, safety, and environmental issues.

Facilities managers are often involved with and are responsible for development and ongoing management of emergency evacuation plans. Facilities are often evacuated for emergency purposes related to fires, explosions, unidentified odors, acts of terrorism, or other threats to human safety. Emergency evacuation plans require development of evacuation routes and training programs that inform personnel and train them to use specific evacuation routes during threatening conditions. In many cases, such evacuation plans are visibly posted and displayed in areas where personnel can see and become familiar with their specific evacuation routes.

Someone must attend to these important needs, and it usually falls within the scope of facilities managers' work to meet these important regulatory requirements. Regulatory compliance, as well as the needs for workplace personnel to know that their health and safety are paramount objectives, combines to increase the stature and importance of high-performance facilities management programs.

Another outcome of organizations' sincere commitments to the health of their personnel has been and continues to be the establishment of fitness centers, physical exercise facilities, and health clubs. These facilities

114

may be pleasant incentives when initially recruiting and hiring personnel, and are often factors in retaining high-quality personnel. Many veteran medical professionals believe that the United States faces a serious medical crisis, that of escalating health care problems and costs caused by people increasingly being overweight and obese. Many organizations are working to combat that situation through providing the facilities, and often some release time from work, so personnel can do the exercise necessary to maintain appropriate weight levels and to maintain overall good health.

Facilities management should provide sponsorship for safety committees, emergency response teams, and environmental groups by chartering and funding such groups in order to enhance the likelihood that services provided by them will be available when needed. In most organizations, leadership in health, safety, and environmental areas typically must come from either astute senior management leaders or it must come from facilities managers. Professional facilities managers' collective contributions to total workplace design and management continue to grow in importance each and every day.

## Health, Safety, and Environmental Continuing Education is Essential

Facilities managers and their work are obviously very unique in many ways. One of the ways they are unique is that they need and can benefit from specialized continuing professional education in so many areas. Expertise is needed in architecture, engineering, construction, maintenance, technology application and use, and many other topics related to facilities development and management. Expertise is also needed in health, safety, and environmental areas if facilities managers are to be capable of providing the leadership in those areas which often must come from them.

All facilities managers are strongly encouraged to create their own personal plans for professional continuing education. Those personal plans might include returning to college as a mid-career or later-career professional to earn a university degree. Or those plans may include attending the IFMA or other relevant professional association conventions, seminars, and expositions. Periodically taking relevant formal courses; aggressively networking with other facilities managers; being a voracious reader who stays current through immersion in industry publications; or thorough preparation for and becoming a Certified Facility Manager (CFM) can all be included in personal plans for continuing professional education. Reality is that the great ones in every profession stay current within their disciplines. Facilities managers need to take the steps necessary to maintain current-to-the-moment facilities management knowledge and expertise.

## Health, Safety, and Environmental "Focal Points"...Facilities Managers

In all organizations, there needs to be someone in appropriate leadership positions—the "focal points"—to coordinate the efforts necessary for making sure that health, safety, and environmental issues are confronted and managed. In large numbers of organizations, those focal points are professional facilities managers.

Facilities managers may not necessarily be the experts or the technicians in many areas of health, safety, and environmental management. However, they need to know where such resources are available and be facilitators of communication between and among various health, safety, and environmental organizations and groups.

As a rule of thumb, facilities managers should defer to the real experts in each of these specialized areas—but never abdicate the responsibilities of making those decisions that emerge as being in the long-term benefit for organizations. It is necessary that health, safety, and environmental professionals work together for the long-term good of their organizations. Facilities managers need to be consistent catalysts who enable that synergy to happen.

## Facilities Management Oversight Responsibilities

Facilities managers should enable specific design, development, construction, maintenance, and operations of facilities that reflect organizations' care, concern, and welfare of all personnel within those facilities. Examples include the design, installation, and operation of heating, ventilation, and air-conditioning systems that enhance indoor air quality.

Proper systems specifications typically include numbers and locations of filters, numbers of air exchanges per hour, and ongoing maintenance to assure that systems are operating at design specifications. Facilities managers often have oversight responsibilities for initiating the design and installation and ultimately the funding of appropriate HVAC systems.

Another example of facilities management oversight is the design, installation, maintenance, and operation of security and other access control systems. Electronic access control systems are often used to replace human security personnel. Fire alarms, water flow alarms, intrusion alarms, motion detectors, close-circuit TV cameras and monitors, and ozone/particulate alarms are commonly part of facilities security systems. Facilities managers often play key roles in designing, selecting, installing, maintaining, and ongoing monitoring of these systems.

In addition to funding the design, selection, installation, maintenance, and operation of security access control systems, fire alarms, and other alarm systems, facilities managers often have budget responsibilities for insurance coverage and fire protection provided by community responders. Such expenditures should be considered during the development of annual facilities budgets.

Facilities interior designs always require attention to the construction and layout of appropriate fire barriers, spill containment capabilities where needed, and appropriate length and configuration of emergency evacuation corridors. These are only three examples of facilities design and layout issues dictated or strongly influenced by existing building features or by building codes, OSHA regulations, or fire and safety regulations. Facilities managers should oversee and assure the consideration of these factors and work to enable funding for resources necessary to meet those objectives.

Code compliance issues do not end within the walls of facilities. Many codes, regulations, and laws impact the development of landscape schemes, roads and streets, parking lots, and exterior green spaces. The amount of surface area devoted to streets, roads, and parking lots will have impacts on the amount of storm water runoff. Consequently, runoff containment ponds may need to be designed and constructed. Some of these storm water runoff issues and containment approaches may also affect neighboring properties. Consideration must be given to the potential impact that runoff may have on surrounding or nearby areas.

Facilities managers also need to be aware of and sensitive to environmental issues related to such things as wetlands preservation, wildlife preservation areas, nature preserves, and other protected areas within proximity to facilities for which they are responsible. Not only are these environmental issues important to facilities managers and their organizations but also to conservationists and others concerned with preserving these resources. Such issues often become emotional issues as well as business issues, and facilities managers and other senior leaders must possess the awareness and skills necessary to address these situations.

Facilities managers should monitor and attempt to ensure the use of good lab practices (GLP) and good manufacturing practices (GMP) which provide high levels of probability that those good practices will ultimately be followed and prevent accidents, fires, explosions, spills, releases to the atmosphere, and other adverse consequences. GLP and GMP must be instilled in workers and monitored on an ongoing basis to assure that applicable safe operating procedures are being practiced.

## *Summary*

Facilities managers, serving in the roles of landlords, should recognize the high level of importance they have for positively affecting health, safety, and environmental issues that impact on their organizations. Implementing the principles of health, safety, and environmental management is in many instances the direct responsibility of facilities managers. In many other organizations, those responsibilities may be vested in a variety of other specialists and leaders but necessitate continual monitoring and oversight responsibilities and periodic actions by facilities managers.

Like so many other areas of facilities management, it is not enough to simply be aware that these issues exist. Facilities managers must know the principles, understand and be able to design solutions, and be the proactive leaders who make sure that these important functions are managed and this critical work accomplished. Be aware of it, study it, understand it, know how to implement it, and support it financially and managerially for the long term.

# Chapter 9

## FACILITIES PLANNING FOR INFORMATION AND TECHNOLOGY SYSTEMS

### *Technology Systems and Facilities Planning are Interdependent*

When designing or building any structure, if we ignore the tools people will need to use within that structure, the structure may never be used in ways that are anything close to its real potential. On the other hand, if people have a tool or an accumulation of tools, they may never maximize the use of those tools if they do not have an appropriate structure or structures within which they can go about their work. While it is not a topic frequently discussed, reality is that planning for the use of technology systems must be consistently intertwined with the planning, design, construction, or renovation of facilities.

If you want to use a robot in a manufacturing process in northern-tier states like North Dakota, and that robot has a water-cooled engine, you will need to keep that robot inside when winter temperatures can hit 30 degrees below zero. If you plan to implement extensive computer networks within a building or campus complex consisting of many buildings, there will be a need to make very specific plans to construct, renovate, and equip those buildings to accommodate all of the cables and related connectivity required to create computer networks.

Virtually every business, government, not-for-profit, and other organization has become incredibly dependent on technology for success. The years of the industrial revolution in the United States following the Civil War which ended in 1865 resulted in a mass conversion from home-based industries to organizations of increasing size within which more and more people combined their efforts to produce products and to provide services. Big looms replaced spinning wheels to manufacture cloth. Water-driven mills replaced hand grinding of grains.

The first assembly lines coupled with specialized labor replaced one person making a product from start to finish. And, it was technology, steadily advancing and continually more sophisticated technologies, that enabled all of these good things to happen. Today's and tomorrow's organizational successes or failures will be heavily dependent on either the successful use of technologies or on inabilities to use necessary technologies.

## *Clarification of the Term "Technology"*

"Technology" can be defined as any manual, automated, or mental process generally using applied sciences to transform inputs into products or services. A dictionary definition of technology is "the terminology of a particular subject-technical language;" or "the science of the application of knowledge to practical purposes-applied science;" or "the application of scientific knowledge to practical purposes in a particular field;" or "a technical method of achieving a practical purpose." Further, technology can be defined as "the totality of the means employed by a people to provide itself with the objects of material culture." "Technological" may be defined as "resulting from improvement in technical processes that increases the productivity of machines and eliminates manual operations or the operations done by old machines."

Today, when the word technology is used, several common interpretations jump quickly into many peoples' minds. Manufacturing personnel tend to think immediately about manufacturing machinery. Medical personnel tend to think immediately about diagnostic and surgical devices. Administrative personnel tend to think immediately about computers, computer peripherals, phone systems, and related office systems. Farmers and ranchers tend to think immediately about tractors, field cultivators, harvesting equipment, and trucks. Law enforcement personnel tend to think about radios, radar devices, computers, databases, handcuffs, sidearms, bulletproof vests, and riot gear. In other words, what jumps to mind as technology to one person may not be the tool or tools that jump to mind for other people.

Technological advancements have continually enabled people to do more and more and then even more with increasingly better technology. Imagine what George Washington could have done to an entire forest of cherry trees if he would have had a chainsaw. The outcome for General George Custer and the U. S. Seventh Cavalry back in June of 1876 in Montana may have been very different if the unit had been equipped with M60 machine guns instead of single-shot Springfield rifles. And, if just one high-altitude Boeing B52 bomber would have been available in 1941, World War II could have been ended decisively and quickly without needing thousands of B17s and B29s.

120

Remember, what surfaces in your mind as state-of-the-art technology may not be the same as what comes to mind for others relative to what is state-of-the-art technology. And, what would be the most appropriate and necessary technology for you to be competitive and successful in some activity or venture may be very different from the technology needed by others to be competitive and successful at what they are trying to accomplish. A variety of technologies may be needed to meet different needs and requirements.

## Technology—One of Five Key Elements of Facilities Management

The right technological choices must be selected and integrated into both senior managements' strategic plans for organizations and into facilities managers' and other operations managers' strategic plans. Leaders and managers in all organizations must be alert to opportunities for improvement, and rapid changes in technology make it a particularly important area for continued focus by facilities management professionals. In Chapter 4 of this book, it was strongly emphasized that the five major components of facilities management and of totally integrated workplace design and management are people, information, process, technology, and place.

The stakes are high for senior management, facilities managers, and leaders at all levels relative to technology selection, implementation, and use. If you are not careful, you could find yourself driving a Ford Model T when you really need a Lear Jet. And, the stakes are high because technological choices that are made will affect the human as well as business and technical aspects of operations and organizations.

## The Generalized Benefits of Technologies

Examples of how and where technologies are being increasingly used to meet business, government, and other organizational objectives include:

*"E-everything"* continues to emerge as a worldwide route to competitiveness and consistent success. E-business, E-government, E-commerce, and the combined use of computers, telecommunications, and related technologies now enables organizations of all sizes located anywhere in the world to potentially compete and be consistently successful. From a big-picture perspective, development or selection and implementation of state-

of-the-art technologies can be and often is the single most critical variable that ultimately impacts the level of organizations' competitiveness and success or in their failure. "E-everything" has become a key element of strategic organizational planning that should be in direct support of organizational objectives and uppermost in the minds of individual professional people and leaders in all organizations.

**Information technologies** merit discussion even before manufacturing technologies because information technologies are now essential in all organizations, including manufacturing. Information technology thinkers and planners should always be directing their efforts toward meeting organizational objectives through the technologies they develop or select and put into use. If we accept the premise that everything IT professionals do should be directed toward meeting organizational objectives, then we need to acknowledge the value of those technologies and thoughtfully prepare facilities that will successfully accommodate their implementation and use.

**Manufacturing technologies** are, of course, critical to the competitiveness and success of all organizations that manufacture anything. It has been said that "building better mousetraps will not make any difference if you can not sell mousetraps." However, many people do not agree with that statement because if you do not build any mousetraps you will not have any mousetraps to sell. Therefore, a reasonable assumption is that if you develop or select and implement state-of-the-art technologies that will enable you to build state-of-the-art mousetraps, you will have high probabilities of being competitive and consistently successful.

CAM (computer-aided manufacturing), sometimes referred to as robotics or as a component of robotics, are commonly used in manufacturing processes of all types. Facilities managers must now be routinely and totally involved with manufacturing professionals for purposes of ultimately providing facilities that enable development and management of technologically-augmented manufacturing of all kinds.

**Computer-modeling technologies for research and development** have emerged to be powerful components of product and services development, refinement, implementation, and use. Computer modeling has also emerged as a key part of achieving competitive advantages because that technology has shortened product development cycles and has shortened time-to-market timeframes. These technologies have also provided manufacturers with abilities to produce products with valued qualities

122

such as greater durability, longer-lasting lifespans, and longer-term positive effects on product users and consumers.

***Industry-specific technologies*** are now available to support and enhance virtually every business, industry, government, not-for-profit, institution, professional, or other entity. The medical profession's use of technology increasingly saves lives and improves qualities of living. The legal profession's use of technology increasingly makes access to full legal services easier than ever. Social services organizations' and professionals' use of technology enables them to meet wider ranges of human needs more thoroughly and more quickly. Architects, engineers, space planners, designers, contractors, community agencies, records managers, administrative managers, and specialists in all fields now have access to technologies that enable them to practice their professions and crafts at higher levels and with more sophistication than ever before.

***Basic business technologies*** now include computer-based order-entry and order-processing systems; accounts receivable, accounts payable, inventory control, payroll, and other accounting applications. Online job applications, multiple benefits administration, and related human resources applications are now in routine and wide use. E-mail, use of word processing, databases, spreadsheets, presentation software, and the myriad of systems utilized for meeting basic day-to-day business transactions and related functions all grow in use every day. Leaders and practitioners in all organizations and endeavors are encouraged to aggressively network for purposes of staying current-to-the-moment in their awareness of and understanding about the technologies which have come into wide use for meeting basic business needs within their own disciplines.

## Facilities Managers' Responsibilities for Planning Technology Systems

Facilities managers must play major roles in planning for information and technology systems design, development, selection, implementation, protection, and use as part of totally integrated workplace development and management. All facilities must be designed with the knowledge that technologies will continue to evolve and change, therefore requiring flexible facilities that will allow efficiently adjusting to that evolution and change of technologies.

Providing technologies, providing for technologies, taking care of technologies, securing technologies, and comfortably working with technologies parallels the need to provide people, provide for people, take care of people, secure people, and to comfortably work with people. Facilities, systems, processes, and methods designed for high-quality workplaces should include effective environments for people and environments for the tools they will need to do their work. Facilities management professionals should keep these issues in mind and incorporate them into their strategic planning efforts.

## Technologies Infrastructure Issues

When designing, constructing, or renovating facilities, consideration must be given to the accommodation of human and technological resources that will be the occupants of and systems used within those facilities. Remember, there must be consideration of both human assets and physical assets management as strategic facilities planning progresses. Optimizing and maximizing values received from those combined assets should be uppermost in the minds of those involved with strategic facilities design, construction, renovation, operations, and management.

Capabilities always need to be built into facilities that will enable distribution of electrical power to meet general facilities needs, to meet workgroup or individual workstation needs, and to provide necessary telecommunications connections. These distribution systems will require appropriate conduit, wire/cable trays, and other means of distributing electricity and telecommunications connectivity to specific locations within facilities. The technologies infrastructure issues discussed in the following paragraphs are not listed in order of importance but rather are presented so that facilities managers remember to consider each of them individually and all of them collectively. These elements are not all inclusive but are representative of technologies infrastructure issues that require specific attention and planning.

*Electrical supplies.* It is not enough to expect that appropriate levels of electricity will always be available when needed. It is also critical that electrical supplies experience absolutely minimal interruptions in the provision of electricity. One way of managing this issue is to develop very close and ongoing working relationships with the suppliers that provide electricity to your facilities. Plan to meet and communicate with them frequently to assure they understand your requirements and so that you understand their abilities to consistently meet your ongoing requirements.

Suppliers of electricity have monitoring systems and procedures in place to determine if there have been spikes and surges in the delivery of electricity. Suppliers use those monitoring systems to determine the overall quality of electricity and their abilities to consistently deliver supplies upon which customers depend. As building systems, computer systems, and other technology systems increasingly demand proportionately more power, it is increasingly critical that suppliers of electricity deliver dependable, stable, and high-quality electrical power to their customers on a consistent basis. With consideration given to the dependency on electricity that supports business operations, it is imperative that facilities managers design, construct, and operate facilities in fashions that assure uninterrupted supplies of electricity.

Among several means of assuring continuous supplies of electricity is the use of UPS (uninterrupted power supplies) systems that usually involve having generators and/or batteries available on a standby basis. Additionally, electrical substations should be located in areas where they can be secured, protected from natural disasters such as floods or wind, and be protected from intentional human or animal damage. Fuel supplies will be needed to run standby generators when their use is required.

It is also important that substations and other components of electrical systems need to be monitored and sized for appropriate response to changing and perhaps increasing demands for dependable and high-quality electricity. Facilities managers must work closely with electrical engineers and facilities operations personnel to assure that electrical systems are designed, installed, and operated at optimum levels.

***Flood protection.*** Obviously, facilities should not be constructed within flood plains without taking appropriate precautions to anticipate potential damage. Water diversion channels, dikes, and other potential flood control measures should be considered, developed, and used where appropriate. Even if water does not rise to levels where it will necessarily reach and enter facilities, it could prevent access from surrounding flooded streets and roads.

Underground cabling systems that provide electricity and telecommunications connections must be protected from potential flood damage. Where electrical supplies and communications systems enter facilities, provisions must be made to safeguard those points of entry. Appropriate placements of sump pumps provide another way of preventing flood damage. Remember, your facility may be high and dry, but your electrical supplier might be threatened by or be experiencing flooding. Facilities managers should work with technology specialists to assure that all technology systems that exist within facilities can continue operating in near-flood or flooding situations.

*Alarm systems.* There are a number of reasons why appropriate alarm systems are either required or are beneficial and need to be installed and used regularly and consistently in the normal course of business. Fire alarms, intrusion alarms, water-flow alarms, temperature fluctuation, and other alarms are among many installed to monitor conditions within facilities. These systems, technologies within themselves, are essential not only to protect the personnel of organizations but also to protect the various other technologies in use within facilities.

Alarm systems are intended to notify emergency responders, community agency responders, and facilities managers that either potential or actual upset conditions have occurred or are probably impending so that appropriate actions can be taken. Facilities managers need to be proactive leaders to assure that alarm systems are in place where appropriate and that they are cost-effectively utilized to assure uninterrupted availability of electricity, uninterrupted abilities to utilize technology systems in place, and to achieve essential security and safety objectives.

*Heating, ventilation, and air conditioning systems.* HVAC systems must be designed to provide essential levels of heating, cooling, appropriate levels of humidity, and good air quality within all facilities. These systems must be able to accommodate fluctuating needs in each of these areas based upon weather conditions and other factors in the geographic areas within which facilities are located. It is also necessary that these systems appropriately dissipate excess levels of heat generated by people and technologies such as PCs, copy machines. Fax machines, and other equipment.

Heat loads will increase as the number of PCs and other technologies are increased within work environments. HVAC systems should be designed to automatically monitor, sense, and appropriately respond to requirements for changing settings. Facilities managers need to work with HVAC specialists to assure that high-quality systems are in place and are appropriately managed on an ongoing basis.

126

***Floor loading capacity.*** Do not build a four-story building out of minimum numbers of 2 x 4s and sheetrock and attempt to park an Abrahms army tank on the fourth floor for purposes of display and atmosphere. If you do that, there could be a very heavy and unwelcome surprise crashing through ceilings and obliterating whatever was below that tank on floors one, two, and three. Likewise, build a four-story building out of minimum numbers of 2 x 4s and sheetrock and then placing high-density mobile steel shelving for paper records storage or inventory storage on the fourth floor could have the same unfortunate results as the Abrahms tank falling through to the lower floors.

Floor load capacities always need to be in the minds of facilities managers and their colleague leaders when facilities are planned, designed, constructed, leased, or renovated. Floor load capacities must be considered when the planning is done relative to what will occupy the space and how much it will all weigh.

High-density filing systems (as mentioned above), high-density multimedia digital data storage systems, computer centers, and other heavy technology or equipment items to be housed within facilities space must be evaluated closely and accommodated in facilities design and construction. Everyone involved in manufacturing and warehousing must diligently remember these same concerns. Proactively planning for heavy weight situations resulting in potential load bearing problems should always be part of facilities managers' thinking and planning.

***Fire suppression systems.*** Many people within many facilities have arguably been lulled to sleep in terms of thinking that the fire extinguisher at the end of the hall means they have nothing about which to be concerned relative to potential fires. Sometimes fire extinguishers are not enough, sometimes water sprinkler systems are not enough, sometimes fire departments do not get there fast enough, and as a result, facilities managers need to provide very knowledgeable leadership relative to fire prevention, detection, and response.

Water fire suppression systems should not be placed in or over computer centers, paper records storage and management systems, archives and museums, or over sophisticated technology systems of many types. As a result, other fire suppression systems—such as dry fire suppression materials, fire suppression gas systems, or dry sprinkler systems—may be individual or collective alternatives to water-based systems in many situations.

127

Prudent planning for many facilities has resulted in installation of fire suppression gas systems as the first-line of defense against fire (as the primary system). The reason fire-suppression gas systems are used is to protect the contents of facilities by extinguishing the fire without dispensing water. Such systems are often backed up by dry sprinkler systems. Dry sprinkler systems are those systems in which water is not released into pipes installed over an area until appropriate alarms trigger that event because primary fire-suppression efforts have failed.

These systems are intended to save the facility if other systems intended for protecting the contents have failed to work. Facilities managers should anticipate and understand the fire suppression technology specifically planned for use within facilities and provide the leadership for designing, installing, and managing appropriate fire suppression systems that will protect personnel, information technologies, other technologies, and facilities.

***Security and access control systems.*** Personnel always need to be protected against dangers that can materialize if unauthorized individuals intending harm are able to enter facilities. Similarly, information technologies and other technology systems in use need to be protected against dangers that are either inadvertent or possible from individuals intending harm.

For example, accidental passage of magnetic components close to or over magnetic digital information storage media can scramble that information by wiping out enough data so that the remainder is unusable. Similarly, incredible amounts of damage can be done in computer-intensive areas if some diabolical individual willfully brings a powerful magnet into those areas and passes them close to recorded media and to computers themselves.

There are, in addition to physical access controls, electronic access controls (as applied to entering computer systems such as unauthorized access to e-mail systems) that should be present. Although facilities managers may not necessarily single-handedly plan for nor manage access to electronic systems, they need to be leaders in working with IT and other technology specialists to plan and implement appropriate electronic access controls.

Other common electronic access controls include the use of machine-readable badges, eye retina scanners, surveillance cameras, electronic door

128

locks, and other such electronically-controlled physical barriers. Facilities managers need to work with security managers and specialists to provide these electronic access controls in addition to other appropriate physical access control and security systems.

Electronic technologies themselves are used to protect other electronic technologies—including databases, e-mail systems, electronic records, data centers, data warehouses, network systems, telecommunications switching equipment, and related technology-supported facilities. These technology protection issues must be addressed in facilities planning, design, construction, renovation, operation, and management.

*Digital information storage media.* As a rule of thumb, the higher the technology of information storage and retrieval media the more vulnerable are the data and records maintained on that media. As a result, a major component in the responsibilities of IT managers and personnel, records managers and personnel, and administrative managers and personnel is that of needing to protect the data and records within digital (electronic) information systems. Part of that protection is needing to appropriately protect the physical digital media on which data and records reside.

High-density storage of data and records on magnetic media of all kinds, optical media of all types, and microfilm media are all physically very heavy. So, thoughtful placement of storage facilities required to house these media is essential. Storage of such media should be done in places where there will be minimal vulnerability to fire, floods, unauthorized human access, unauthorized electronic access, and other forms of intrusion.

Those information storage media should also be maintained in physical areas where they are easy to monitor and to alarm in ways that allow quick responses to potential intrusion or damage. Facilities managers should work hand in hand with IT managers, records managers, administrative managers, and information users to design, locate, construct, operate, and manage appropriate facilities for use, storage, and management of such information media.

*Paper forms storage.* Paper forms continue to be one of the most widely used types of business documents. Several industries and professions, such as medicine, insurance, and government at all levels continue to have very large volumes of paper business forms in use. As a result—even in our age where so much good has been accomplished through the development of computer-based information systems—most business, industry, government, and other organizations have large volumes of paper business forms with which they must cope and manage. Facilities designed for technologies planning and use should also include well-planned provisions for managing inventories of paper business forms.

If your computers and high-volume printers are located in your headquarters building, you probably would not want to store your inventory of blank paper business forms in your aircraft hanger located five miles away. Some business forms must technologically be acclimated in terms of temperature and humidity control with the printers on which they will be processed. As a result, methodical planning with IT and colleague information managers will be important for facilities managers so that paper business forms are available where, when, and in the conditions that they are needed.

Security of many blank forms is often an issue. You probably would not want to store blank copies of the company's paychecks on a pallet in the hallway of the warehouse with the open loading dock that is next door to the work release area of the county jail and across the street from the bar. Facilities managers should work with IT managers, records managers, forms managers, other administrative leaders, and users to plan appropriate storage locations for paper forms supplies in order to provide the availability, inventory control, appropriate physical locations, environmental conditioning, and security necessary for effective business forms management.

***Telecommunications cable systems.*** Providing support for technology systems requires thoughtful and appropriate provision of physical distribution capabilities to hold electrical wires, coaxial cables, fiber-optic cables, and other needed communications connections. In addition to the suggestions shared earlier in this chapter, there are other factors related to the use of telecommunications network systems. One consideration is that of how to accommodate such systems in the design of individual workstations.

Providing telecommunications network wiring/cabling to buildings does not finish the job. Distributing wiring to individual workstations is also required. Some facilities distribute telecommunications systems through channels or troughs built into floors. Other methods use raised flooring systems through which telecommunications wiring/cabling can be delivered to any locations where needed. Many other facilities require the dis-

130

tribution of these utilities through ceilings or commonly known as overhead distribution systems.

Manufacturers of most work stations have been aware of and have tried to address wire/cable distribution within their furniture systems. However, some cable/wire systems are easier to accommodate within workstations than are others. The numbers of wires and cables distributed to a workstation may be limited by the size of wire management channels available or the size (thickness) of those channels. Another factor is that copper wiring can be bent in order to be threaded through wire management channels on workstation panels while fiber-optic cables usually cannot be bent to the same extent as copper wire without breaking.

Additionally, some voice and data lines must also be shielded from electrical lines and from crossing and touching one another. Planning for telecommunications cable distribution and electrical distribution must be done with the concern in mind that they may not all be able to be distributed through the same conduits.

Distance (physical proximity) and physical locations are also important factors in planning telecommunications systems and facilities. Some wire systems experience degradation in signal strength over longer distances so signal-repeaters or comparable technologies may be needed. Other organizations will elect to implement satellite-based or microwave-based systems in order to cope with distances between facilities that need to be connected.

Facilities managers need to factor all of the elements relative to telecommunications cable systems into their planning as they work with IT and other specialists to plan, design, construct, operate, and manage these systems. If this leadership does not come from facilities managers, then these essential functions often are not accomplished as thoroughly and as professionally as necessary within organizations.

***Accommodating information technologies through appropriate facilities design.*** There are several methods commonly used to assure continuous operation of information and other technology systems. Often primary systems are backed up with redundant systems, meaning that entire primary systems are methodically duplicated at other physical locations and are thus available essentially on a standby basis in the event they are needed to replace primary systems. Typically, redundant systems are housed in additional facilities geographically separated from primary facilities and systems by distances of at least a few miles.

In other situations or in addition to self-maintained in-organization redundant systems, some organizations elect to contract with outsource service provider organizations commonly referred to as hot-site companies. These outsource companies provide online real-time computer systems backup services coupled with storage of digital records in order to accomplish vital data and records protection objectives.

Ergonomics—which integrates the use of space, technologies, furniture, and the physiological factors of light, color, sound, and temperature to meet the psychological and physical needs of personnel in work environments—is important not only to human productivity but to good management of technology infrastructure issues. As previously discussed in Chapters 7 and 8 of this book, the science of ergonomics has evolved in large part because many technologies have been implemented in many workplaces.

Some of the earliest origins of ergonomics came from combinations of human factors analysis coupled with needed technology systems to design cockpits and aircrew spaces for World War II-era fighter and bomber aircraft. When a World War II fighter pilot needed to fire his machine guns, he had to be able to keep his eyes focused on the enemy aircraft and still reach and manipulate his gun charger switches and his triggers. Designing those cockpits (workplaces) and aircrew workplaces around the needs of those pilots and aircrew members were critical to their individual and collective safety as well as to get the ultimate job done—win that war.

Applications of information technology have heavily influenced applications of ergonomics in workplace environments, specifically highlighting the need to build workplaces around the work to be done. Good cockpit designs helped win World War II. Good workplace designs help organizations be highly competitive and successful.

The installation of information technology in today's workplaces has had significant influences on the design and installation of lighting systems, HVAC systems, acoustics, and on selections of colors and finishes for workplace furniture and total environments. Information technology has heavily impacted the design, configuration, size, and arrangement of individual workstations and group workplaces. Requirements for storage and management of information technology media must be considered in

132

the planning, design, configuration, and installation of personal workstations as well as for totally integrated workplace design and management.

Telephone closets, network server rooms, and copying and fax areas all represent work areas that must be accommodated within the planning, design, construction, and operation of facilities. Facilities managers should carefully factor these space and utility requirements into the planning of totally integrated workplaces.

## *Summary*

The last several years have seen a major evolution in computing technologies, and that evolution has increasingly impacted the work of facilities managers. The 1960s, 1970s, and most of the 1980s were years of highly-centralized organization-wide computing functions (often referred to then as data processing or MIS (management information systems) involving heavy use of large mainframe computers. Starting in the 1980s, more and more increasingly powerful desktop computers (PCs) permeated office environments and began to be cabled together into client/server computer networks. This phenomenon gradually de-emphasized the need for physically larger computer centers in favor of physically decentralized desktop computing.

To facilities managers, that meant that rather than satisfying the needs of one DP manager and her or his staff relative to facilities for computers and computer-related technologies, now it became necessary to meet those needs for large numbers of desktop computer users. Instead of building large centralized computer centers, it was now necessary to physically distribute electrical supplies and communications connections throughout entire facilities. Workstation designs were impacted as they needed to accommodate computers and computer peripherals.

Most facilities managers accepted the challenges associated with the evolution of computing systems architectures. They implemented the solutions necessary to achieve successful physically decentralized client/server computing that now characterizes a majority of today's organizations. The years ahead will continue to see the successful implementation of information technology systems and all technology systems depend heavily on the leadership and direction provided by professional facilities managers working closely with IT and other technology leaders and specialists.

# Chapter 10
## *FACILITIES MANAGEMENT AND RECORDS MANAGEMENT: A PARTNERSHIP*

### *Records are the Memory of Organizations*
### *Records Must be Professionally Managed*

### *A Real-World Case from 3M Company*

There had been a close working relationship between Facilities Management and Records Management at 3M for nearly 30 years. A new office building was being designed in the early 1970s at the company's headquarters in St. Paul, Minnesota. During that process, it became very clear that their partnership would be very valuable to the ultimate effectiveness of that facility. Other than for the corporate records storage space set aside for use within the facility, the building had been designed, constructed, furnished, and occupied without any involvement from the company's Records Management Department.

The Facilities Management staff and the Records Management staff soon collectively discovered while the records storage space was being designed that the requirements of both organizations needed to be defined, understood, and resolved as the building moved toward occupancy. It became very clear that:

➡ Facilities Management was constrained by the dimensions of the building caused by the dimensions of the property on which the building was being constructed. Length, width, and height were limited by several factors related to the location of the building.

➡ Facilities Management was constrained by a construction budget and a budget for final occupancy of the building.

➡ Facilities Management was constrained by the number of tenants that wanted and/or needed to occupy the facility. Space was very carefully and conservatively allocated to each anticipated tenant including the space allotted for a corporate records storage facility and other records storage and management systems.

➡ Facilities Management did not have enough money budgeted to accommodate the special fire detection, fire suppression, and security requirements needed for a records storage and management facility.

➡ Records Management was constrained by not getting as much space as needed, anticipating the use of traditional storage methods, to accommodate projected records storage growth.

➡ Records Management was also constrained by the fact that several important records management facilities-related issues were not taken into consideration during the building design and, as a result, needed to be addressed and resolved very quickly as the scheduled date for building occupancy was rapidly approaching.

Records Management, because of the limited space allocated for records storage and management, ultimately decided, in an attempt to assure accommodation for eventual records storage volume growth, to install a large high density mobile shelving system that would allow for substantially more efficient utilization of the allocated space. However, the decision to install the large mobile shelving system raised several significant issues for Facilities Management to address.

Floor loading capacity immediately became an issue because each 63-feet long and 10-shelf high isle of mobile shelving when loaded with paper records would weight approximately 27 tons. And, it was anticipated that the allocated space would accommodate approximately 30 aisles of the mobile records storage shelving. Isles to be used for storing microfilmed records and computer media would potentially weigh more than 27 tons each. As is often the case, this kind of floor loading requirement meant that the records storage facility would need to be located on the basement floor (lowest level) of the building. This location also proved to provide the best access to shipping and receiving docks as well as offered better fire and security protection.

Height of the basement (lower level) facility became an immediate issue because it was determined that to maximize the space and use the mobile shelving system most efficiently, 15 feet of clear height was necessary to provide optimum value. This requirement impacted the overall design of the basement space and also had an impact on the overall height of the building.

136

Layout of the shelving was important because of needed provision and dispersion of light into each isle. Each row of lights had to be installed in positions to disperse light into each isle as it opened for access to the boxes and other containers of records. Records Management personnel needed adequate levels of light in order to read the labels and contents of the records storage containers. Electrical supplies also had to be provided in specific locations in order to provide appropriate power for electric motors that moved the mobile shelving units.

To ensure state-of-the-art protection of the records stored and managed within the new facility, a dry Halon gas fire suppression system was ultimately selected, designed, and installed. Halon gas systems are often the first line of defense against fire. If, for some reason, a Halon system does not extinguish a fire and preserve the records, then a backup sprinkler system can activate and douse the space with water in an effort to save the remainder of the structure.

The new records storage and management space also required a climate-controlled environment. Facilities Management and Records Management ultimately worked together to identify, specify, and provide a state-of-the-art climate control system that would assure optimum protection of all information storage and management media housed within the new facility.

## A Facilities Management-Records Management Partnership Provided Solutions

All of the lessens learned from this 3M facility design and construction experience illustrated the myriad of issues that Facilities Management and Records Management can individually and collectively identify, evaluate, and for which they can develop some kinds of solutions. They could then design, install, pay for, and effectively manage those solutions into the future. This project became an extremely positive and valuable turning point at 3M in the relationship between the Facilities Management and Records Management departments.

## There is More to the Story

A second story to come out of the design, construction, furnishing, and occupancy of the 3M facility was the selection of file cabinets that were purchased for the new facility. Records Management was not initially involved with Facilities Management in the evaluation of the filing equipment ultimately selected, purchased, and used by the tenants in their new building.

A few months after the occupancy of the new building, the Corporate Records Manager at the time—Dan Brathal—was asked to help a tenant in the new building with the development of a microfilm system to handle the storage of records in the tenant's department. As was often the case, the tenant had heard about the space-saving benefits of microfilm and wanted to use that media to make room for additional paper records.

A records analyst reviewed the records to determine if they were covered by an appropriate records retention schedule. The analyst determined how the records were being used in an effort to determine which media would be most appropriate for storage, retrieval, distribution, and protection of the information. The records analyst, working with the tenant, determined the value of the information, the length of time the information should be retained, the frequency of retrieval, and the number of users requiring access to the information.

The analyst also determined the frequency of distribution, the security needed, and then was able to compare storage alternatives and select the media that would be most effective for those records. The objectives of this work were to determine what records existed, how long they needed to be retained, what the frequency of reference would be, where the records should be stored, and what the most appropriate records media would be. That work was followed by initiating the elimination of those records that, according to the records retention schedule, no longer needed to be retained.

When the records analyst arrived in the client department, it was discovered that some of the new file cabinet drawers would not open. File cabinets with rollout drawers are routinely equipped with safety interlocking devices that prevent more than one drawer from being opened at the same time. If more than one drawer is opened, too much weight can be displaced off the center of a cabinet and it may topple over onto a person using it. It was immediately clear that the interlocking devices in some new file cabinets were sometimes not functioning properly, and this immediately caused serious concern by the records analyst.

The Records Management organization, in addition to helping their client develop an organized records retention and management program for that unit's records, contacted the Facilities Management group and requested a meeting to discuss the potential for working together to provide better filing systems for all 3M tenant organizations. Initially, the Facilities Management group had some reservations about the potential impact on their corporate furniture standards program and on their purchasing contracts with suppliers of filing equipment.

Both Facilities Management and Records Management soon agreed that there was much potential for positive impact on the company if both groups would work together to assess, and adjust if appropriate, the buying practices in place across the company for procurement of filing equipment. This new partnership was a huge breakthrough for providing the most state-of-the-art filing systems and equipment for all future building and remodeling projects.

In subsequent building and remodeling projects, Records Management reviewed the records management practices of all tenants before they were relocated into new or renovated space. Records Management:

➡ Checked for up-to-date records inventories;

➡ Checked for up-to-date records retention schedules;

➡ Provided assistance in discarding records that were no longer needed thus avoiding the cost of personnel time and resources required to move records that could be destroyed;

➡ Determined which records were to be retained, which records should be sent to inactive storage in the Corporate Records Center, and which records needed to be retained within the tenant department or departments;

➡ Worked with tenants to determine what and where records should be retained and to determine what media should be used to capture, safeguard, store, retrieve, and distribute the information contained in the records; and

➡ To determine what type, how many, and what configuration of file cabinets tenants would need in their new locations to appropriately store and manage the paper and other records media in use.

# Outcomes of the 3M Construction Experience

All of these efforts were designed to optimize investments in people who were using the records and records management systems, to minimize space consumed by records storage and management, to optimize investments in filing equipment and supplies, and to minimize floor loading stress. Additional objectives were to optimize investments in environmental controls, optimize investments in utilities, provide records and information in ways that enable better and faster decision making, improve productivity, improve competitive advantages, and enhance the aesthetics of tenant workplaces.

An exciting result of the 3M building design and construction experience was that 3M building and remodeling projects from that point forward were furnished with standardized fixed-shelf filing cabinets for filing systems using end-tab folders that were color-coded when appropriate. File cabinets were also increasingly configured with accessories appropriate for storing and managing a variety of media. The cabinets featured doors and locks to provide secure storage of information. Buying power was also enhanced and leveraged for purchasing file cabinets and supplies.

Beginning with the Facilities Management-Records Management partnership, when tenants submitted purchase orders to buy additional file cabinets, Facilities Management would not approve the orders until Records Management did an assessment of the need. They determined if there were ways—through adherence to retention schedules, transferring records to the Corporate Records Center, or use of alternative records media (film or digital), to avoid purchasing additional filing cabinets.

The Facilities Management-Records Management partnership resulted in virtually no additional file cabinets being purchased over the course of the next several years for tenant utilization. The results were records being managed much more effectively through appropriate application of records retention principles. Less money was spent on filing equipment, less space was consumed by unnecessary or inactive records, there was much less clutter in workplaces, and higher levels of security were maintained for the information contained in the company's records.

# Records Management Fundamentals for Facilities Managers

Ask business owners, executives, managers, and people at any level in today's workplace environments, and most will tell you that the volume of records continues to increase at unprecedented rates. Administrators and personnel in all levels of federal, state, provincial, and local government offices say the same thing. The number of e-mails, electronic records, paper documents, and other records continues to grow. Data and more data! Paperwork everywhere!

If all of these records are not managed and handled appropriately, they can be deleted, lost, or misplaced. Often they are difficult or impossible to retrieve and use. The results are lost business opportunities, upset customers, costly delays, disappointed managers, and frustrated personnel. More critical is the result that owners, executives, administrators, managers, and personnel may be forced to make decisions based on inadequate information. Even scarier is the possibility of lawsuits and adverse financial consequences of litigation.

The numbers of electronic records are growing exponentially because of continually increasing dependence on more powerful and versatile computers and on easier-to-use software and systems. Our dependence on e-mail, availability of information from the Internet and the Web, conversions of paper forms to electronic forms, and steady growth in the use of electronic imaging systems all add more electronic records.

Paper records are still increasing in number and literally flood many offices. Some recent estimates indicate that between 50 and 80 percent of the records in many organizations continue to be paper documents. A result of this continuing information explosion is a tremendous need in most organizations for learning how to manage and use electronic, paper, and other records more appropriately and effectively.

Unfortunately, in many organizations, the proper management of records has not been a high priority. Perhaps, management did not find records issues important or exciting enough. More likely, they saw records management as a cost to the organization's bottom line. But attitudes have really changed in the recent past. Records management has become a major topic of discussion in corporate boardrooms, in executive suites, and in the media. Large and growing accumulations of electronic, paper, and other records are of major concern.

The astronomical accumulation of electronic records is increasingly causing IT professionals to realize that newer, faster, and more innovative systems need to be developed and implemented. And, all records, especially electronic records, have become prominent in litigation. Often in the heat of litigation and the legal discovery process, requested records cannot be found and the resulting cost is huge to search for, retrieve, review, and provide needed information from potentially decades of records.

The attacks by terrorists on the World Trade Center and the Pentagon on September 11, 2001, instantly caused many business owners, corporate leaders, government administrators, and leaders in other organizations to wonder about the readiness of their organizations' disaster recovery and vital records situations. By 2002, media attention focused on the obstruction of justice prosecution against Arthur Anderson LLP. A jury ultimately found Anderson guilty of destroying potentially incriminating Enron Corporation audit records while a federal investigation was in process.

In response to this case and other corporate abuses, Congress approved the Sarbanes-Oxley Act of 2002 which was signed into law by President George W. Bush on July 20, 2002, to add government oversight of public accountants and establish corporate responsibility for financial reporting. Executives and leaders in all organizations now increasingly recognize the potential risks and penalties for neglecting their records management programs.

Records management has finally emerged as a significant concern of corporate officers, upper management, legal departments, and information technology groups and is no longer just an on-going concern of records management professionals. There are legal, economic, and practical reasons to clean up the mess, establish an appropriate records management program, and properly manage all of an organization's records—paper as well as electronic.

A records management program is neither a luxury nor an option. All organizations need a records management program to fully comply with the law. Most organizations need a records management program to help clean up the messes. Additionally, all organizations need a records management program as a base for appropriately managing records and information resources.

142

# What are Records and What is Records Management?

"Records" are recorded information, regardless of medium or characteristics, that have been created within or received by an organization and that have been or are used in the accomplishment of work, as evidence of its activities, or because of the information contained. Within computer-based information systems, a record is more narrowly defined as a collection of related data fields. Books, computer-readable media such as disks and tapes, microforms, paper documents, photographs, videos, voice or sound recordings, or other documentary materials—again, regardless of physical form or characteristics—are common types of records.

"Electronic records" are defined in several ways, including information stored in (on) machine-readable media. Practically speaking, today—in the eyes of the law—if you have recorded information, it can be subpoenaed, and it will be considered a record. Unfortunately, little thought is typically given to how records can be successfully managed when organizations are new and small. However, as organizations grow and prosper, the volumes of recorded information (the records) typically grow quickly.

"Records management" is defined as the professional management of information in the physical form of records from the time records are received or created through their processing, distribution and use to placement in storage and retrieval systems until either eventual elimination or identification for permanent archival retention. It is the management of information through the life cycle of records. Records management can also be defined as a professional management discipline that is primarily devoted to the management of document-based information systems and to the management of recorded information required in the operation of organizations.

Much credit for the development of professional records management goes to the U. S. Government. Congress passed a General Records Disposal Act in 1889. The National Archives of the United States was established in 1934. In 1943, the National Archives developed the first records disposition schedule and its implementation was authorized by the Records Disposal Act. In the late 1940s, President Truman established the Commission on the Organization of the Executive Branch of the Government, which in turn created the Task Force on Paperwork Management to evaluate records management within government. A result of that work was the establishment of the Records Management Division within the National Archives in 1949 and the establishment in 1950 of the Regional Records Management Service.

The professional field of records management started as an extension of the archival profession and, within the United States, originated at the National Archives. Professional records management was also badly needed in private business and industry. The National Records Management Council was established in 1947 to extend records management principles, developed largely within government, to private business, industry, and other organizations.

The American Records Management Association was founded in 1955, became the Association of Records Managers and Administrators in 1975, and evolved to be today's ARMA International which is now the world's international association for records management professionals. ARMA International has over 10,000 members in approximately 40 countries who are members of approximately 130 chapters. ARMA membership is subdivided by areas of interest into ISGs (Industry Specific Groups) which enable records management professionals to network with other professionals within their respective industries. Access the resources of ARMA International—including an online "Bookstore"—by going to the association's website at www.arma.org.

The Institute of Certified Records Managers (ICRM) was established in 1975 and administers a program for professional certification of records management professionals. Candidates for certification must possess necessary education and experience requirements and pass a stringent six-part written examination administered by the ICRM. A practicing Certified Records Manager (CRM), to maintain certification, must demonstrate continuing education achievements. For applications and information about the ICRM and the CRM examination, go to the Institute's website at www.icrm.org.

## The Records Management Situation in Many Organizations Today

What is the current records management situation in organizations where you work or are a stakeholder of some kind? Almost everyone recognizes and agrees that records are the memory of organizations and that there is a need for managing records well. Most agree that the information explosion is continuing and that volumes of electronic, paper, and other records are steadily increasing. All agree that we are experiencing exponential growth in the volume of e-mail and other electronic records. Unfortunately, almost everyone also admits that they personally do not know or are not sure about how records can be managed most effectively in today's organizations.

A major problem in so many organizations is the fact that the worldwide educational level about professional records management is extremely low. The vast majority of today's business owners, senior corporate executives, business managers at all levels, senior government officials and administrators, and other leaders—including virtually all professional facilities managers—have never taken formal records management courses offered at a university business school or in other management development settings.

Most senior leaders do not understand professional records management. Most do not know how successful records management programs can be developed and managed. Most are not accustomed to providing leadership, management support, funding, and staffing for records management. As a result, there are many organizations of all sizes in corporate, private, government, and not-for-profit organizations that do not have adequate records management programs.

Another major problem continues to be extensive decentralized control of records within organizations. For example, in many city government situations, fire department leaders are often left on their own to determine which records they need; which records should be electronic, digital, paper, film, or other; to determine how long records are to be retained; and to determine when and how records should be eliminated. Similarly, leaders in many police departments are being left on their own to make those same decisions relative to their records. Situations in many corporations are very similar. Often, managers and personnel are being left more or less on their own to resolve records management problems and challenges as effectively as they can.

Decentralized control of records generally should be abandoned in favor of establishing senior-management supported and centrally-managed organization-wide records management programs. Just as organizations will benefit in so many ways from having organization-wide high-performance facilities management programs, organizations benefit in so many other valuable ways by establishing appropriate organization-wide records management programs. Many aspects of the work performed by professional facilities managers and records managers overlap. Their organizations will benefit in many ways from a FM-RM partnership where these professionals work closely together. Reference the 3M example presented at the beginning of this chapter.

An especially troublesome problem, with major implications for facilities managers, is the fact that most organizations continue to keep records too long. As results, efficiency suffers, personnel costs rise because of people wasting time searching for records between and among those that should have been eliminated, excessive amounts of physical space ends up being used to house records, filing equipment and supply costs often escalate, and there is unnecessary legal exposure. Today, it is just as easy to experience adverse legal consequences because of records being retained too long as it is because of records having been eliminated too soon.

Many organizations are operating with unprotected vital records. Vital records are typically those records that are either essential for organizations to operate or records that are necessary to meet legal, ethical, or moral obligations to customers, clients, constituents, employees, and other stakeholders. There are statistics from the U. S. Small Business Administration obtained between 1975 and 2000 documenting that 93% of U. S. organizations that lost their vital records either failed immediately or attempted to resume operations but failed within two years.

If that statistic does not support the fact that records are the memory of organizations, it is unclear what could make that point more strongly. An essential responsibility for the Facilities Management and Records Management partnership is that of identifying organizations' vital records as part of business continuity planning processes and then taking appropriate steps to back them up and secure them.

Today's sophisticated global positioning systems (GPS) and other technologies allow us to instantly find exact locations of objects in space, planes in the air, and places or objects on earth. Why then is it so difficult in many offices to instantly find file folders and records in paper filing systems? Reality is that filing systems for paper records in many offices are out-of-control messes. A major problem continues to be heavy dependence on old traditional pull-drawer filing cabinets. They consume excessive amounts of floor space while selecting and utilizing alternative shelf-based systems comparatively saves so much floor space and capitalizes on the potential of unused vertical space in offices and other facilities.

146

Selection and implementation of appropriate filing systems equipment now requires the expertise of both records managers and facilities managers.

In many organizations, inactive records, many often dating back to the founding dates of organizations, are currently being maintained in inappropriate situations and are being allowed to deteriorate. Basements, old warehouses, old city jails, dismal storage rooms, unused offices, parked semi-trailers, rental storage garages and other spaces are used as storage spaces for inactive records. Today's organizations need the combined expertise of records managers and facilities managers working together to develop appropriate systems and facilities for the management of inactive records.

Finally, most organizations are not yet utilizing and capitalizing on the benefits of technologies (records management software, electronic records systems, digital records applications, and electronic imaging systems) that are now readily available to them. Often, it is primarily a matter of education—a need to learn about these systems and about their potential implementation and use. Most organizations today are not yet successfully integrating their IT and records management programs; and, as a result, several technologies with excellent potential for achieving many benefits and returns are still not in wide use.

Readers are encouraged to take thorough analytical looks at the current records management situation in organizations where they are stakeholders. Benchmark where those organizations seem to be in relation to what is commonly seen today in business, industry, and government. Start the process of determining what leadership needs to be provided and which steps need to be taken in those organizations to develop appropriate records management programs.

## Benefits and Return on Investment of Records Management Programs

Organizations will benefit in many ways from the establishment of centrally-managed organization-wide records management programs:

→ ***Increased Executive, Managerial, and Operational Effectiveness.*** If leaders and professionals at all levels have almost instant access to complete and accurate records, they can perform their functions, do their work, and take care of the people they need to serve. If information in records is not available, decisions and administrative functions are delayed and usually become more costly.

➡ ***Measurable Increases in Staff Productivity.*** If staff members have almost instant access to relevant, current-to-the-moment, complete and accurate records, then they can meet the needs of customers and clients and do their work effectively.

➡ ***Legal Defensibility.*** In today's legal environment, organizations are vulnerable to as many adverse judgments because of records being retained too long as they are for eliminating records too quickly. It is no longer reasonable, cost-effective, or managerially appropriate to retain records "just in case." It has never been as critically important to manage records retention processes appropriately and well as it is today.

➡ ***Compliance with Federal, State, and Industry-Specific Legal and Regulatory Requirements.*** There are now over 12,000 U. S. federal and state laws and regulations that impact on record-keeping requirements. Appropriate retention management enables avoiding or minimizing costly fines or other penalties as well as reducing risks in civil litigation and government investigations.

➡ ***Improved Customer Service.*** Improved customer service is a major benefit of high-quality records management programs. Reality is that if records (electronic, paper, or other) can be almost instantly accessed, then people needing service can be served.

➡ ***Reduced Operating Costs.*** Reduced operating costs can be achieved through reducing labor requirements for the creation, organization, distribution, retrieval, use, and management of information.

➡ ***Reduced Storage Requirements.*** Less space is needed for records equipment and supplies proportionate to the volumes of records maintained when records managers and facilities managers combine their expertise to develop appropriate programs.

➡ ***Reductions in Records Volume.*** Implementation of records management programs often results in the elimination of 30 to 40 percent of organizational records quite quickly. The transfer of 30 to 40 percent more records from active to inactive systems or conversion of those records to other media (film or digital) can often follow. And, many organizations can then operate efficiently with 30 to 40 percent of the initial records volumes that remain. There can be substantial reductions in records volumes in virtually all of today's organizations.

➡ ***Coordinated Planning for Development of Electronic Records Programs.*** When paper records are managed appropriately, electronic records programs can usually be developed faster and less expensively and with better results.

## *Go Electronic (Digital) if Practical*

Readers, owners, managers, and decision-makers are encouraged to go electronic with as many of their organizations' records and information systems as possible. The greatest volume of records in many organizations continues to be paper documents, and that needs to change. Electronic records are created whenever someone creates an e-mail message or uses word processing, database, spreadsheet, or other computer system to enter data or create electronic documents. Electronic records are also created when existing paper or other records are scanned and digitized to convert them into electronic form.

Major advantages of electronic records include achieving abilities to provide faster service because of the ease and speed with which electronic records can be accessed. Increases in staff productivity come quickly by decreasing the dependence on cumbersome uses of paper records. Processes can be re-engineered, several people can work on records at the same time, records can be captured or created in many places for central processing and made available over the Internet or through other computer networks, and vital records can be easily backed up to enable business continuation in the event of disasters or terrorism.

Rapid expansion of and success with computer-based information systems and electronic records has spread through all industries and professions. Readers and leaders are strongly encouraged to aggressively network and quickly learn what computer information systems, computer uses, and electronic records applications have emerged as best practices within their own industries and professions.

## Strategies for Starting a Records Management Program

What are the steps that need to be taken in most organizations to establish centrally-managed organization-wide records management programs? Recommended practical strategies include:

➡ Quickly and methodically survey the organization to determine the current records management situation. Take photos, creatively gather facts about current records management costs, determine how much facilities space is being consumed by records, and interview personnel at all levels to identify records management problems, volumes, issues, and opportunities.

➡ Secure a strong commitment from owners, executives, managers, and other leaders for starting and supporting a records management program. Senior management commitment and support will be the biggest factor in whether or not the program succeeds or struggles.

➡ Designate an appropriate individual to be the organization's records manager, and place that manager and program on a peer level with the organization's IT/IS manager and program. Stress that the IT/IS manager and records manager will be expected to create and nurture a relationship in which they can work closely together and combine their expertise to accomplish good records and information management systems. Go electronic (digital) with as many applications and records as practical and use computers to augment management of records on all media.

➡ Carefully select and designate "records coordinators" in each of the various departments or units of the organization. Selected from among present personnel, these key persons will be involved in implementation within their units and be representatives to the organization-wide records management program.

➡ Inventory the organization's records, preferably developing online lists of the types of records (records series) that exist on all media within the organization. Follow precedence within your own industry or profession about how to most efficiently conduct that inventory. If the records of any organization are really going to be managed, an inventory process is essential to determine what records exist on all media.

150

➡ Develop and implement a legally valid records retention schedule covering records on all media. Do the necessary legal research, build an internal consensus, and determine how long records of all types are to be retained in active systems, in inactive systems, and when they will be either eliminated or identified for long-term or permanent retention. Secure legal counsel and senior management approval. Implement the retention schedule; delete, transfer, or eliminate records retained beyond their retention times; and manage that process regularly and consistently in the normal course of business.

➡ Establish a standing Records Management Committee consisting of the records manager, records coordinators, IT/IS manager, facilities manager, and representatives from accounting, finance, administrative services, legal, and selected other departments or units. Meet periodically to assess progress, identify and prioritize records management needs, and to discuss processes for the successful advancement of the records management program.

➡ Follow through to implement the other components typically included in successful organization-wide records management programs. Implement electronic records systems and applications whenever possible. Identify and protect the vital records. Upgrade to state-of-the-art shelf-based filing systems for active records. Find the inactive records and work with the organization's facilities manager to achieve appropriate storage and management of those records internally if storage is not outsourced to a commercial records center company. Implement digital or microfilm imaging systems when appropriate to further decrease the dependence on paper records. Select and implement records management software. Take steps to identify and manage records of eventual archival value.

## *Resources About Professional Records Management*

A wealth of high-quality records management resources (records management seminars on CD-ROM, books, online services, industry reports, white papers, and professional associations) are now available. Very few senior leaders in any profession or field have ever taken formal records management courses—resulting in the fact that a lack of knowledge about professional records management continues to be a huge problem within business, industry, government, and most organizations of all kinds. A majority of organizations today still do not have organization-wide records management programs, often primarily because nobody really knows or understands how an appropriate program could be developed and managed.

A resource just introduced in November of 2003 is a new 8-hour CD-ROM "Establishing and Managing Successful Records Management Programs" video seminar. Presented by Dr. Mark Langemo, CRM, this video seminar provides the comprehensive records management education needed as a base for strengthening existing records management programs or for developing and managing new programs. The CD set comes in an easy-to-use format that will install quickly on your PC-compatible computer. For information about this CD records management seminar, contact Information Requirements Clearinghouse, Inc. at 303-721-7500 or go to the IRCH website (www.irch.com).

Facilities managers and others who are concerned about records management within their organizations are encouraged to acquire the practitioner-oriented and highly-practical "Winning Strategies for Successful Records Management Programs" book written by Dr. Mark Langemo, CRM, and available from Information Requirements Clearinghouse (go to www.irch.com and click on "NEW Winning Strategies...").

Records retention legal research software, records retention books, and related legal resources are available from Information Requirements Clearinghouse, Inc.; 5600 South Quebec Street, Suite 250-C; Greenwood Village, CO 80111; 303-721-7500; www.irch.com. Especially valuable are the "Retention 3.0" and "Legal Requirements for Business Records: The Electronic Edition" software resources which can be used for purposes of doing the research necessary to determine which laws and regulations apply to your organizations' records and to generate legally-valid records retention schedules.

An excellent comprehensive new online resource providing electronic records management information to anyone everywhere anytime on the legal, technical, and operational issues of electronic records management is available from Cohasset Associates, Inc., at www.MERresource.com. Cohasset also sponsors the annual MER Conference (Managing Electronic Records) in Chicago.

As a reminder, ARMA International is the international professional association in the field of records and information management. ARMA International has over 10,000 members and over 130 chapters—the majority within the United States and Canada. Membership is open to ARMA's "ISGs" (Industry Specific Groups) enabling members to network with records management professionals within their own industries and professions. ARMA's superb annual conference, excellent online bookstore, periodic webinars, association-sponsored seminars and conferences, and an annual buyer's guide are among the resources available.

Books and other publications from ARMA International include expertise about records management fundamentals, the value and business case for records management, records management in smaller businesses and organizations, and information management for multinational corporations. Resources are available about managing e-mail, managing electronic records, managing records retention, vital records management, managing inactive records, electronic document imaging, microfilm systems, filing systems development and management, records management in government organizations, meeting HIPAA requirements, and managing records for ISO 9000 compliance.

Contact ARMA International at 13725 West 109th Street, Suite 101; Lenexa, KS 66215; 800-422-2762; or go to the association's website at www.arma.org.

## *The Value of a Records Management-Facilities Management Partnership*

Organizations of all sizes within business, industry, government, not-for-profit, and other organizations can now benefit more than ever before if facilities managers and records managers combine their expertise and work together to achieve multiple objectives and benefits.

➡ Records managers contribute significantly to organizations through participation in the development of appropriate and efficient records and information management programs. They also develop systems in which workers can be more productive thus requiring fewer workers to operate organizations and less space needed to accommodate them.

→ Records managers can plan and oversee management of records retention processes that result in reduced volumes of records needing to be retained in facilities.

→ Records managers can contribute to the planning, selection, and implementation of state-of-the-art filing systems equipment, media, and supplies for active records storage and retrieval systems.

→ Records managers can contribute to protecting organizations from fines, legal costs, and adverse consequences of litigation related to facilities design, development, and utilization (documentation for regulatory requirements).

→ Records managers can provide leadership essential to the appropriate management of inactive records—typically a major consumer of space in facilities of virtually all organizations.

→ Records managers can contribute in many ways to the development and maintenance of aesthetically pleasing workplaces.

→ Facilities managers can optimize the value of spending for the planning, design, acquisition, construction, and utilization of built space.

→ Facilities managers can optimize space utilized for information storage and management within both active and inactive records systems.

→ Facilities managers can optimize the value of spending for records and information storage, retrieval, protection, and distribution facilities, systems, and equipment.

→ Facilities managers contribute significantly to their organizations through participation in the planning, management, distribution, and use of well-conceived records and information management systems. Those systems can have significant impacts on infrastructure design and costs such as for floor loading capacity, electricity, lights, heat load, cooling capacity, acoustics, telecommunications cables, fiber optic wiring, satellite and microwave equipment, phone closets, environmentally controlled spaces, and telecommunications switching centers.

Several related issues relevant to the facilities management and records management partnership are also discussed in other chapters of this book that are devoted to technology, office layout and design, and other topics. A strong records management-facilities management partnership has the potential to make total workplace development—and the work lives of facilities managers and records managers—much less complicated and much more successful.

## *Summary*

"Records" are information, regardless of media or physical form, that have been created within or received by an organization or individual and that have been or are used in the accomplishment of work or as evidence of activities. Practically speaking, today—in the eyes of the law—if recorded information exists on any media, it can be subpoenaed, and it will be considered a record. Records management is the professional management of information through the life cycle of records. Records management is also defined as a professional management discipline that is primarily devoted to the management of document-based information systems and to the management of recorded information used within organizations.

Unfortunately, in many organizations, the management of records has not been a high priority. More recently, steadily increasing volumes of records, concerns about terrorism and about potential losses of vital records, and several startling illegal events have caused records management to become a major topic of discussion in corporate boardrooms and in the media. All organizations need a records management program as a basis for providing high-quality customer service, for being in legal compliance, for managing effectively, and for positively impacting the financial bottom line.

The responsibilities of facilities managers often overlap with those of records managers, especially in the provision of filing systems for paper records and in the management of inactive records. Facilities managers and records managers are encouraged to develop close working partnerships in order to combine their individual expertise to accomplish both high-quality records management and high-performance facilities management for their organizations.

Use the contents of this chapter as a basis for becoming familiar with common records management situations today. Learn the fundamentals of how to establish and manage organization-wide records management programs. Become familiar with the professional resources about records management available from ARMA International, Information Requirements Clearinghouse, and other sources. Learn about the Certified Records Manager (CRM) designation and about the potential for CFMs to partner with CRM colleagues. Learn the values and the benefits that can come to organizations as the result of a facilities management-records management partnership.

# Chapter 11
## POTENTIAL AND CHALLENGES OF TELECOMMUTING

### Telecommuting Provides Access to Qualified Workers — Many Do Not Wish to Hold Traditional Full-Time or Part-Time Jobs

"Telecommuting" is a variation of work scheduling in which employees work away from traditional office settings—usually at home. They typically utilize telecommunications links from their computers and other technologies at home to their employers' systems. An often-debated topic, telecommuting has its advantages and proponents—as well as disadvantages and detractors. The co-authors' intent in this chapter is that of presenting the topic, some of its pros and cons, and to identify those issues that any organization with telecommuting employees is likely to encounter at some point.

Career optimists, like the two co-authors of this book, think of telecommuting primarily because of the exciting potential it provides for both employers and employees. And, the co-authors are not alone in their thinking in that telecommuting has become an increasingly hot topic since its use accelerated in the late 1980s. Years ago when research and development, manufacturing, marketing, administrative, and computing functions were traditionally highly centralized and remote-access technologies were in their infancy, telecommuting often was not a widely viable alternative. However, as portable and highly connectible computer-based and other technologies grew into wide use, the possibility of more and more employees working from home or at locations other than their companies' headquarters grew in viability.

### Potential Advantages of Telecommuting

**Potential telecommuters often like the idea of working at home.** Work when you want to work. Sleep longer each morning. Have the option of staying up later at night. Take a nap when you want to take a nap. Keep the kids at home instead of sending them to daycare. Get more quality time with the children. Cut down on daycare expenses. Avoid

157

time-consuming and frustrating commutes. Save money now being spent on gasoline. Cut down on the miles put on personal vehicles. Save money now spent on parking. Save some money now spent eating out. Avoid much contact with overbearing supervisors or boring co-workers. Be freer to participate in church and other volunteer activities. Have the flexibility to play in a bridge group or schedule extra rounds of golf. These commonly held "off-the-cuff benefits" of telecommuting tend to be uppermost in many employees' thinking.

*Employers tend to think about the potential of saving* workspace if telecommuters would work at home or at other locations. Reduce time listening to people complain about commuting. Cut some costs for workstations, technologies, furniture, and related overhead. Some scheduling issues are minimized when fewer people come to work at set periods of time. Utilities costs for electricity, heating, and cooling may be reduced. Save on daycare facilities and services offered at some workplaces. Social concerns such as reducing pollution, saving highway wear and tear and saving energy are altruistic benefits. Cut down on the sizes of parking lots needed. Reduce the food services that must be provided. Reduce custodial costs. Enjoy the public relations values of being seen as human-sensitive family-oriented employers. Maybe even make more money.

*In times of chronic shortages of qualified personnel,* employers offering telecommuting alternatives may be able to hire and employ highly-specialized and well-qualified personnel who otherwise may not be available to them. For example, young attorneys who have small children and who aspire to be at home a high percentage of the time may be ideal solutions to some smaller organizations seeking in-house legal counsels. And, software development companies seeking creative computer programmers may be able to recruit and employ young programmers who want larger amounts of time at home with their small children.

*Capitalizing on the many advantages of employing disabled persons* can be good for those who want and are able to do many kinds of basic to highly sophisticated professional work. Many of such people could be available to employers if they would be allowed to work from home or other locations instead of needing to physically commute to employers' traditional workplaces. Racially diverse, ethnically diverse, and culturally diverse workforces can also be created if all of the employees do not need to live in narrowly centered geographic locations.

158

**Some types of jobs and positions may lend themselves to the work of telecommuters** more than other jobs and positions. Jobs performing transactions may be excellent candidates. Someone can sit at home in Fingal, North Dakota, or Baldwin, Wisconsin, and take telephone orders originating from catalogs for the J. C. Penney Company. Airline reservationists may be able to book flights and services from virtually anywhere. Computer programming, computer help desk, and related IT functions can often be performed very successfully by telecommuters. Other jobs that require collaboration and teamwork may not be as conducive to telecommuting. Readers are encouraged to aggressively network within their own industries or professions to research what types of jobs and positions are proven to have high probabilities of success for telecommuting personnel.

## Social Issues and Challenges of Telecommuting

**Social isolation may grow as a negative aspect of telecommuting** as amounts of time in physical proximity to workplace colleagues is minimized. The loss of face-to-face contact with co-workers and supervisors can result in adverse consequences as basic as being largely forgotten about or being taken for granted. "Out of sight, out of mind" is a concern that telecommuters may not initially anticipate but that often eventually becomes an issue. Over a period of time, being out of sight and out of mind may adversely affect career advancement potential. Many people, including the two co-authors of this book, are routinely energized intellectually and emotionally because of having ongoing interactions with current and former colleagues and associates.

**Senses of belonging and being one of the team are subject to being diminished** when employees spend large amounts of time apart from co-workers. Baseball relief pitchers who spend large amounts of time in the bullpen may get to know the other relief pitchers, but they may not feel they have much to do with many other teammates down the line in the dugout. Getting to know your co-workers, teammates, colleagues, and fellow professionals usually means learning about their families and gaining insights into their lives—all of which often leads to individual happiness and higher group morale. Human beings, via their very nature, are social creatures that have inherent needs, at varying levels, to interact with other people.

159

**Collaboration between and among co-workers and colleagues is often less possible** when many of those individuals are telecommuters. Collaboration is often the source of larger numbers of good ideas, solutions, initiatives, and projects—generated from the abilities of multiple individuals feeding off each other and playing off each other to collectively stimulate thinking and creativity. Collaboration is typically a propellant for new ideas. Too much time alone tends to foster introspection and becoming set in certain ways while collaboration usually expands the number of alternatives people will consider. When telecommuting is implemented on larger scales, then planned times to bring telecommuting co-workers and colleagues together usually becomes very important to the long-term success of the organizations involved.

**Communications lapses may occur when many co-workers and colleagues work at home** or at places other than employers' locations. As a result, there are not as many visits around water coolers, in hallways, in parking lots, or in cafeterias. Disconnection from the grapevine sometimes leaves employees wondering whether or not they are on the inside of what is going on within organizations. When difficulties develop between spouses, lack of communication is often identified as part of the problem. When difficulties develop between parents and their children, lack of communication is often identified as part of the problem. When difficulties develop between management and personnel, lack of communication is often identified as part of the problem. There is also a visual component of communication including the ability to see co-workers' faces, read their body language, and sense meanings from their innuendoes.

## Business Issues and Challenges of Telecommuting

**Common and perplexing business issues associated with telecommuting** include insurance questions, potential insurance liabilities, potential workers compensation problems, and challenges of workplace development and management. If employees work at home and visitors to home offices are injured during visits, are the employers' insurance providers liable or are the employees' own insurance providers liable? If employees themselves suffer carpel tunnel or other injuries deemed by them to be associated with work for their employers, then are workers compensation claims justified or not? If employees select their own home workplace furnishings and technologies and then are electrocuted by computers

160

they selected, are employers ultimately responsible because computer use was required—or not?

*Air quality, heating, and cooling* are often major issues in employer workplaces. But what if telecommuting employees working at home develop pneumonia because their workplace is freezing? Was it the employer's responsibility or the employee's own responsibility? These are representative and certainly not a complete list of common and perplexing business issues associated with telecommuting. Senior leaders in all organizations, including facilities managers, need to collectively address and resolve these issues for their organizations prior to any extensive involvement with telecommuting.

*Furnishing and equipping home offices* (or other home work-places) often brings several issues into question. For example, who buys the furniture—the employer or the employee? Who buys the computer, printer, scanner, copier, fax machine, and the water cooler—the employer or the employee? If employers do not make those purchases, then should financial grants or allowances be provided by employers to employees for acquisition of those needed workplace components? Will employers purchase and provide office and other workplace supplies? Who will pay for the postage? Although some of these may seem like smaller issues, when multiplied by several or larger numbers of telecommuting employees, they can grow into issues of magnitude and of significant costs.

## Records Management and Information Systems Challenges of Telecommuting

When employees of any organization work at home or in locations other than at their employers' sites, huge issues are that of who owns the records and who will appropriately manage that recorded information? Chapter 10 of this book is devoted to the development of high-quality organization-wide records management programs. This is a topic of extreme importance to facilities managers and records managers because of their common involvement in housing and managing inactive records and in the installation of equipment for active filing systems. Records are the memory of organizations and those records need to be managed in accordance with well-established records management program policies and procedures. Managing records when some or many employees are telecommuters can be very challenging.

3M, for example, had long maintained—and enforced—a policy that the company owns and will retain internally within the company all corporate databases. That long-standing policy was reinforced at 3M, in part, after hearing strong rumors that another major company had moved to out-source its human resources functions—only to learn that the outsource provider was allowed access to an information system that enabled them to access confidential records and information from the host company. What steps were taken to assure that the contracted provider did not dupli-cate, share, or damage the integrity of the database? The potential legal vulnerabilities of such a situation could be enormous.

In our litigation-intensive environments, organizations can get into just as much legal trouble by retaining records and recorded information too long as they can get into trouble by deleting or eliminating records and information too quickly. Again, as stated earlier in this book, it has never been as important to appropriately manage records retention functions according to legally valid records retention programs and schedules as it is today. Ultimate disposition of records and recorded information in home and other offices is typically a very sticky issue and must be done in accor-dance with established retention programs and practices.

Information systems (IT) challenges associated with telecommuting often focus first on what technologies are to be used by individual telecommut-ing employees. Also, ensuring compatibility for employers' systems, main-taining the capabilities to integrate from home and other offices into employers' information systems architectures and protocols, and the abil-ities to comply with IT policies and processes will be very important to long-term success. Security of computer-based information systems, protection against viruses, protection against using home and other offices as possi-ble points of intrusion into employers' information systems are all IT chal-lenges to be resolved.

Telecommuting employees often are also isolated from a myriad of resources that would be valuable to them in the performance of their work. How is reference and research to be done within organizational active paper filing systems, inactive records systems, company libraries, and other infor-mation and reference repositories that may be housed at employers' facil-ities? Telecommuting issues such as these are among many that facilities managers must participate in resolving.

## *Summary*

Telecommuting is a variation of work scheduling in which employees work away from traditional office settings, usually at home. Telecommuting has its advantages and disadvantages. Many employees like the idea of potentially working at home and realizing a number of individual, family, and cost savings advantages. Many employers like their potential to recruit and retain specialized personnel who may not be available to them otherwise—and to cut space needs, reduce many other costs, and achieve other advantages in the process.

Social issues involved with telecommuting include the potential for social isolation, loss of teamwork, less possibility of benefiting from ongoing personnel collaboration, and having to overcome lapses in communications. Business issues associated with telecommuting include insurance, liability, environmental, and the creation and maintenance of appropriate workplaces.

Records management issues focus primarily on the challenges associated with management of records retention in decentralized telecommuting environments. Information systems challenges focus on the issues associated with keeping telecommuting employees appropriately equipped yet connected to systems of their employers. Some jobs and positions are much more suited to the potential for successful telecommuting than others. Facilities managers, along with members of senior management, need to be involved with telecommuting decisions because they are fundamental to successful totally integrated workplace development and management.

# Chapter 12
## ASSURING BUSINESS CONTINUITY AND RESUMPTION

### *Implications of Operating Facilities in a Global Economy*

Tune into any newscast, read any newspaper, browse through nearly any magazine and you will often learn of unfortunate and tragic events happening around the world. Earthquakes, hurricanes, floods, fires, storms, political unrest, civil unrest, acts of terrorism, disease, famine and war are among the events that cause upset conditions surrounding the lives of people. Tragedy can strike in many forms from among an extensive list of possible disasters.

Normally, our first reactions to such incidents are to think about the toll these events take on human beings. It is appropriate that we think first about the pain, devastation, and suffering experienced by victims and others who are impacted. Additionally, the impact of devastating natural and human-created tragedies may be felt for long periods of time and in the lives of individuals, businesses, institutions, and all organizations alike. There is no way human beings can prevent some of the most devastating natural disasters. And there is nowhere to hide from some results of actions taken by diabolical people whose intent is to terrorize the world. Facilities managers, all professional business managers, and other leaders must be prepared to manage an appropriate response to events that upset our lives and our organizations.

More than at any previous time in history, today's businesses, institutions, governments, and organizations of all types are being influenced by global events. Extraordinary levels of trade and commerce are happening across international borders. Commerce of all types is being conducted through technologies and devices that sit on earth, fly above the earth, orbit the earth, float on water, and lie on the floors of oceans. Effective utilization and ongoing maintenance of all these technologies and interactive devices often heavily depends on peaceful and cooperative international partnerships and agreements. As the global commerce network expands into new reaches of the earth, so does our vulnerability to disruptive events.

## Business Continuity Stakes are High

Global competition has increasingly raised the level of vulnerability to and the potential impacts of unexpected disruption of normal operations. As businesses, institutions, agencies, and organizations of all types around the world become more and more dependent on sophisticated technologies, the economic impact of those technologies also continues to increase. Global trading partners depend on continuous supplies of goods and services and when that supply of goods and services is interrupted, every organization in the chain of business partners may be negatively effected. Consequently, interruptions in normal business operations may cause a ripple effect that threatens the continuous smooth operation of any or all business partners involved in the supply chain.

As the world evolves into a more strongly networked and technologically integrated economic system, disruptions to normal business operations become a growing concern. A natural or human-created catastrophe occurring anywhere in the world may have devastating results elsewhere in the international economic system. An earthquake in Mexico may have huge effects on the United States and Canadian economies by disrupting abilities to fulfill orders negotiated through NAFTA agreements. A flood in South America may impact the European economy by disrupting the flow of food supplies and other South American-produced products upon which others have become dependent. Likewise, a terrorist event in the Middle East may have negative impacts on the people and economies of whichever countries' people, facilities, or other resources were attacked.

Within a global economy, there usually are too many circumstances that evolve to be on the fringe or outside of our individual control. In a supply chain that is spread all over the world in different geographic regions, in different political systems, in different cultural environments, and in places where individual values may vary, systems for delivering consistently high-quality goods and services often become more fragile and difficult to manage. It is imperative that facilities management professionals, working with other professionals in numerous management disciplines, work together to address the consequences of potential minor or major interruptions to normal business operations.

Publications and other media contain too many examples of organizations that were literally put out of business by some kind of interruption to normal business operations. There are other examples of organizations that were devastated by a disruptive event and had to struggle very hard

166

to rebuild a supply chain that allowed for the consistent delivery of high-quality products and services.

## Milliken & Company's Great Response to a Disaster

3M had, in addition to buying from several other carpet suppliers, historically been a large customer of Milliken & Company, a major supplier of high-quality commercial carpeting and related products. Tragically, the Milliken factory that produced carpet for 3M burned to the ground on January 31, 1995. Within a few days of that disaster, 3M's Facilities Manager received a personalized letter from Mr. Roger Milliken, Milliken's CEO and Chairman of the Board, first reporting that no Milliken employee was killed or injured by the fire.

Mr. Milliken went on to explain the origin and extent of fire damages to the Milliken carpet factory. He also added a step-by-step explanation of how Milliken was going to assure a continuing supply of carpet for 3M and for other Milliken customers. His letter contained a stated commitment to rebuild the factory and to include advanced state-of-the-art carpet manufacturing technology in the new facility.

Mr. Milliken closed his letter with a sincere "thank you" for 3M's business. He personally assured 3M that the products and services they had come to expect from Milliken would continue to be provided and would be continually improved. Mr. Milliken's personal response to that disaster gave confidence to 3M and other customers that his company's facilities would be restored and that Milliken's ability to provide products and services would continue into the future.

Roger Milliken's letter and his explanation of how 3M's business relationship with Milliken & Company would be preserved and strengthened was a major source of reassurance at a time when 3M was extensively using Milliken products in major facilities renovation projects. Milliken's response to the disaster preserved a valuable partnership with 3M and probably did the same with many of Milliken's other customers. Milliken & Company went on to restore effective carpet production operations in a new factory facility that contained state-of-the-art technology and arguably produced even better carpet than was produced before the tragic fire.

## Hacker-Created Headaches!

Computer hackers can really cause havoc and disruptions! Numerous stories have been written and told about computer hackers who have invaded both public and private computer systems. Hackers have stolen information about the personal lives of many people and about the business practices of public, private, and other organizations. Hackers have created and planted insidious computer viruses that then disrupted computer operations, sometimes around the world.

Computer crime continues to escalate as a fast-growing type of crime and mode of terrorism with scary potentials to disrupt the lives of individuals and organizations alike. Again, potential dangers present risks for organizations and individuals that depend heavily on computer systems and technologies. Organizations rely on having high integrity computer-produced information that can be used in decision-making processes. With today's dependence on computer systems, disruptions of normal computer operations can be extremely costly to all parties that depend on such technologies.

## Some Disasters Do Not Initially Appear to be Disasters

Disasters may occur in places and in ways that may not or that seldom initially come into our minds as disasters. Do you agree that the alleged accounting scandal at Enron was a disaster? Do you agree that those circumstances constituted a disruption of normal business operations within Enron and elsewhere? Do you also agree that literally thousands of individual lives were impacted by those questionable accounting practices? Simply stated, all of us must be dedicated to assuring that continuous, effective, legal, ethical, and successful operations will be possible within businesses, agencies, institutions, and organizations of all types.

## What is Business Continuity Planning?

As this chapter was being written, wild fires were raging across the landscape in Southern California. More than 100,000 residents were evacuated from their homes. The fires had already consumed thousands of homes, and 50,000 more homes continued to be threatened. Entire towns had been destroyed. At least 20 people had been confirmed as killed, and

168

many more were expected to be found in burned-out automobiles — killed while trying to evacuate their homes.

Estimates of damage ranged in excess of $2 billion, and the fires were still raging and not yet under control. More than 700,000 acres of landscape were nothing more than charred remains of trees, homes, and other structures. These fires have been described as the most devastating fires in the history of California. How would people, businesses, and organizations recover from such devastation?

Many businesses and other organizations were closed because of the fires and because workers could not get to their workplaces. Roads and highways normally used by commuters had been closed. Air traffic control centers had been closed causing interruptions of normal airline service. Business travelers could not get to their destinations to conduct business. All these closings had a widening effect on the conduct of commerce and throughout the economy of the region. Tragically, these disastrous fires had devastated individuals as well as businesses.

"Business continuity planning" is the thoughtful process of anticipating potential disruptions and identifying the people, equipment, facilities, business processes, information, data, and other items that are vulnerable to potential interruption of normal operations. Also included is planning for maintaining continuous operations and for the resumption of operations that become interrupted by a natural or human-created disruption of normal business activities.

Business continuity planning also involves the development of preventive practices that help avoid unplanned interruptions of normal operations and activities. A comprehensive and effective business continuity plan will include processes for identification of vulnerabilities and priority business functions, prevention of interruptions, responses and reactions for mitigation of interruptions, resumption, and restoration of normal effective operations.

Business continuity planners often struggle to define an appropriate balance between how much effort and money should be spent on disaster prevention and contingency planning as compared with how much effort and money could be lost or spent on the resumption of operations with no business continuity plan in place. Additionally, business continuity planners must determine how much money should be spent on prevention, mitigation, backup, and recovery before the cost of those items becomes greater that the costs of potential losses.

Determination of how much time and money to invest in contingency planning is much like trying to determine how much money should be spent on insurance. Most individuals struggle with the question of how much insurance coverage of various types should be carried in their personal lives. Similarly, businesses, government agencies, institutions, and other organizations of all types often wrestle with how much money should be spent on disaster prevention, mitigation, and recovery. There is no one right answer, of course, that applies to all situations. Answers must be developed that thoughtfully, effectively, and most appropriately serve the best interests and the most logical recovery requirements for each individual organization.

## How Extensively Should Prospecting for Vulnerabilities Take Place?

Business continuity planning has historically centered primarily in data processing, information systems, and information technology operations. IT professionals have often been more diligent about applying the principles of business continuity planning or disaster recovery planning than their counterparts in other parts of organizations. While it is very appropriate to safeguard IT operations, it is equally important to assure that all other organizational operations be protected to the extents reasonably possible and that those other operations should also be restored as quickly as possible following an interruption.

A careful and thoughtful business continuity planning process, also known in many organizations as "risk assessment and management," should lead to the identification of prioritized critical operations. With critical operations identified, planners should proceed with development of specific plans for the prevention, protection, use of restoration resources, and to the allocations and prioritization of those critical resources required for restoring critical operations. Prioritizing the allocation of resources is an especially important component of business continuity planning.

A business, government agency, institution, or organization of any type may have literally dozens of points of vulnerability. Such points of vulnerability may exist both internally and externally to an organization and to its facilities. Some points of vulnerability typically are easier to address

170

and manage than others may be. Ultimately, it will be necessary to prioritize those vulnerabilities and prioritize the allocation of resources necessary to address those needs.

Good information is a common thread and requirement that exists in all effective business continuity and restoration plans. A well-developed and comprehensive records management program is a vital component of an effective business continuity plan. Vital records identification and protection are critical elements of appropriate and successful records management programs. Records that are required to assure continuous operations typically include personnel records, articles of incorporation, real estate records, production specifications, and other asset records. Organizations may also identify and safeguard other records vital to their operations.

For example, while accounts receivable records may be vital to assure continuing cash flow and income, accounts payable records may not be vital to an organization experiencing an unplanned business interruption. Those parties to whom money is owed (accounts payable) will undoubtedly provide their records of payments due. This information management issue, among many others, reinforces the need for facilities management professionals, business continuity professionals, and records management professionals to work together in a strong partnership to assure appropriate identification, protection, and management of vital records and information that would be necessary for continuous and effective operations.

## A Business Continuity Planning Model

There are many components that should be included in an effective business continuity plan. Those components should generally be arranged in three primary categories. **Preparation** of the plan requires careful thought and arrangement of steps to be included in the plan. **Prevention** includes identification of steps needed to minimize risk and damages that could be potentially caused by disasters. **Reaction** requires development of processes necessary for effective response to incidents and steps necessary to achieve a return to normal operations.

## Plan Preparation

The first component of a business continuity plan, the preparation phase, is really where contingency planning and documentation should take place. The prevention planning phase is done in effort to avoid disasters and to provide for operational stability. The reaction planning phase is designed to assure that operations recover from a disastrous interruption.

When proceeding into the preparation phase, it is important to initiate the plan preparation process with the objective of identifying the appropriate stakeholders and then gaining their understanding for the importance of and their support for a comprehensive business continuity plan. All stakeholder organizations should provide input to the development of an effective organization-wide plan.

With the planning process initiated and all stakeholder organizations identified, all associated organizations should individually and collectively conduct a risk evaluation to determine operational areas of vulnerability to interruptions and the estimated potential cost of such interruptions to normal activities. The risk analysis should include looking for potential failures in facilities, laws and regulations, policies, processes, equipment, markets, suppliers, human resources, financial reserves, and other assets critical to operating the organization.

Workers on the top floor of the Sears Tower in Chicago may not be concerned about potential floods. However, the company's telecommunications services may have cables running underground in Chicago and elsewhere. Those cables could be put out of service by floods. *Identify your assets, know where they are located*, and *know their potential vulnerabilities.* Assess the level of potential risk to organizational assets and determine how much money should be spent to protect those assets necessary to continue or to restore normal operations.

Having performed a risk identification and evaluation, organizations should then determine the potential impact that work stoppages or disruptions would have on their operations. This step is often referred to as a business impact analysis. Again, areas of risk should be identified and then assessed to determine the extent to which failures would impact the overall operations of the organization.

Some pharmaceutical companies are obligated by law to assure a continuous supply of certain drugs that protect the health and lives of people with life threatening illnesses or diseases. If those drugs cannot be supplied because of either a short or lengthy business interruption, the impact on those businesses, and more importantly, on the lives of those who depend on such drugs, could be devastating. Businesses, government

172

agencies, institutions, and organizations of all types must identify, analyze, and quantify the potential impact on their operations if suddenly unplanned and disastrous interruptions occur.

By this point in the preparation of a business continuity plan, all appropriate stakeholders should have been identified and, working together, they should have collectively taken steps to initiate the business continuity planning process. Planners should have identified potential risks to the organization, assessed those risks in effort to determine which of them present the highest potential for causing interruptions to operations, and they should have identified and analyzed the potential impact that interruptions could have on the ability of the organization to operate. When these steps are completed, it should then be time to identify, assess, and develop the appropriate business continuity strategies.

Development of business continuity strategies should involve a high-level look at the facilities, people, systems, processes, technologies, equipment, services, suppliers, distributors, markets, and perhaps, other stakeholders that combine to enable continuous operation of an organization. In looking at these components, it is important to assess them with the intent that only the critical elements will be covered in the business continuity strategy. While all elements of an organization are important to continuous operations, it is much more effective to identify and prioritize only the critical elements that need extraordinary safeguards in order to stay in business and maintain operations. Separating the important elements from the critical elements and then protecting the most critical elements is done most effectively with a strategic thinking and strategic planning approach.

Building on the plan preparation hierarchy, with the planning process initiated, the risk evaluation completed, the business impact analysis done, and the business continuity strategy developed, then it is time to begin communicating these principles to the workers in operating units that ultimately need to develop and manage their components of a business continuity plan. It is critical that all business units be informed and thoroughly "sold" on the importance of a well coordinated and all-inclusive plan that personnel will routinely support and keep updated as requirements change. Marketing the principles and the value of business continuity planning at all levels in the organization will have huge impact on the success or failure of the planning effort.

After marketing the principles of business continuity planning and making personnel aware of the value of such plans, then it is time to perform final development and documentation of the plan or plans. It is sometimes a bit difficult to determine the best method for documenting business continuity plans. Typically, many plans are documented on paper and stored in three-ring binders in somebody's workstation or office. While this approach can be successful, it requires considerable discipline to assure that plans are updated each time they require changes. For example, call lists are difficult to keep current as people move around in organizations, as responsibilities change, and as other changes occur that require updating the plans. Plans documented on paper will become outdated quickly unless someone is given responsibility to keep them current and then is held responsible for making sure that work gets done.

There are a number of software packages now available that are designed specifically for purposes of documenting business continuity plans. Such software offers a structured format that can be used effectively and consistently throughout entire organizations. Software may often appear to be more costly than paper for documenting plans, but paper documentation is also more difficult to keep updated and current. It is important to compare the cost, consistency, currency, convenience, and effectiveness trade-offs between electronic-based systems and paper-based systems available for documenting business continuity plans.

The last step in preparing and deploying a business continuity plan involves training personnel in how to execute the plan when and if necessary. Along with training, routine testing and exercising of a plan will enhance its reliability and that of the personnel responsible for maintaining and executing the plan. Overall quality of a plan will depend largely on how currently the plan is maintained and on how well individuals are trained to successfully implement it.

In summary, **preparation** of an effective business continuity plan should involve:

- ➡ Initiating the planning process.

- ➡ Performing a risk evaluation throughout the organization.

- ➡ Performing a business impact analysis.

- ➡ Development of a business continuity strategy.

174

- Informing personnel about processes for developing business continuity plans.

- Development and documentation of organization-wide business continuity plans.

- Establishment of a routine training and testing program to assure effective execution.

## *Prevention of Business Interruptions*

The second step in plan development should involve a well conceived and effective business continuity plan that contains many components designed to prevent upset conditions from happening. When business interruptions are prevented, many areas of cost will be avoided. Maintaining normal operations is considerably easier than restoring operations that have been interrupted and then having to return them to normal operations.

Prevention of unplanned business interruptions should begin with the establishment of a senior management supported policy that outlines the value and the importance of preventing harm to an organization's personnel as well as harm to normal operations. Today, competition is so intense that even short interruptions of normal operations can threaten the survival of even the strongest organizations. A well-conceived policy that creates a strong mindset for prevention of interruptions can engage all organization personnel in preserving their jobs and enhancing their success.

Along with a strong policy directed toward prevention of business and operational interruptions, a carefully designed set of standardized practices, standardized procedures, and standardized operating processes will add strength to any program designed to prevent unplanned business interruptions. In many cases, there are also advantages associated with standardized equipment, computers, telecommunication networks, software, and other tools employed in today's workplaces. Familiarity with and integration of compatible systems can add assurances that processes and operations will run as smoothly as possible. Again, operating, equipment, and systems standards should be included in documentation of the plans.

With policies and standards established and deployed, it is important to develop clearly written guidelines for supporting the policies and utilization of the standards. Development of operating guidelines should include an operations assessment as sophisticated as flow-charting or sometimes called process mapping. Flow charting business processes often identifies opportunities for changes in operating guidelines that will strengthen procedures and enhance the reliability of current systems.

Similar to the plan preparation component, the policies, standards, and guidelines of the prevention component must also be conveyed to all organizational personnel. Awareness training and explanation of the plan are critical to the level of understanding by those who will be responsible for maintaining and executing a business continuity plan if it becomes necessary to do so. It is important for all personnel to know what they can do and what they must do to prevent interruptions to normal business and other operations.

In the area of information technology, it is particularly important to develop a computer and related technology architecture that allows for integration of different hardware, software, and peripheral components. Recognizing the fast pace of change in computer technologies, constant vigilance must be paid to the compatibility issues that can either enable or endanger the smooth and continuous operation of IT systems. A technology architecture that ensures continuous operations is a critical element of a successful interruption-prevention protocol.

Like the preparation component of a business continuity plan, the prevention component must also be developed, documented, and implemented. Established policies, standards, guidelines, and technology architectures must be documented and conveyed to all personnel who will be responsible for management and maintenance of their related portions of the business continuity plan. The extent to which stakeholder personnel accept responsibility for and properly maintain the plan will assure the adequacy and successful execution of the plan.

Earlier, the pace of technology changes in the IT environment was raised as a challenging element of business continuity planning. But a good business interruption prevention plan would not be complete without a plan for managing the rapid changes taking place in workplace technology. As time goes forward from the development, documentation, and implementation of a well-constructed business continuity plan, managing and integrating changes becomes an increasingly more challenging and an increasingly more important element of the plan. A strong change management process must be part of well-conceived business continuity plans.

And finally, like the plan preparation component, the prevention component of a good business continuity plan must have maintenance discipline included to assure that plans will enable businesses to meet their objectives for continuous operations. Plans must be monitored and adjusted as necessary to assure that they will enable businesses to effectively and efficiently continue operations. Again, monitoring the prevention plan is much like testing the plan as called for within the plan preparation process.

The primary elements of an interruption **prevention** plan include the following:

➡ Establishment of an organization-wide interruption prevention policy.

➡ Creation of standards for procedures, processes, practices, equipment, computer hardware, software, and other workplace tools.

➡ Provision of awareness and training for personnel that must be responsible for development and maintenance of appropriate business continuity plans.

➡ Development of a technology architecture that will enable integration and continuous operation of computer hardware, software, and peripheral equipment.

➡ Development, documentation, and implementation of interruption prevention plans.

➡ A process for managing changes and updates to the interruption prevention plan.

➡ A process for ongoing monitoring and compliance of the interruption prevention plan.

## A Plan for Reaction to Business Interruptions

The third component of a business continuity plan relates to the development of an appropriate reaction to potential business and operational interruptions. Referring back to the early stages of plan development (the plan preparation component), the risk evaluation and the business impact analysis will identify the critical processes, equipment, systems, documents, and procedures that must be protected with the prevention and reaction components of the plan.

When business interruptions occur, the initial response to an interruption will have huge impacts on how quickly the cause of the interruption is identified, the continuity plan is implemented, and the upsetting situation is mitigated. Those organizations with well-conceived, well-documented, and well-tested response plans will benefit in many ways and are in a much better position to stay in business than those organizations trying to respond without previously developed response plans. It is critical that organizations of all types respond to upsetting interruptions as quickly, efficiently, safely, and effectively as possible. To accomplish that objective means having a plan developed, procedures documented, appropriate equipment and supplies conveniently available, people trained, individual responsibilities carefully defined, communication systems established, and a fierce determination to quickly mitigate causes for any interruption.

After an interruption is mitigated and the threat of additional damage and disruption is minimized, it is crucial to quickly resume some level of normal business and other operations. Resumption of operations may mean quickly setting up business in alternative facilities or somehow resuming the use of equipment and supplies or contracting work and services from other sources. The objective of resuming operations as quickly as possible is to avoid losing customers and the revenue those customers generate. Maintaining cash flow is critical to the ongoing survival of any organization that experiences an unplanned interruption of their operations. A business resumption element is a very important aspect of an effective business continuity plan.

Obviously, resumption of operations is a critical step toward getting back to a normal level of business. Often, in order to resume normal operations, it will be necessary to retrieve information, backup systems and equipment, specifications, policies, personnel, and other resources from offsite locations. It is critical to recover all resources and systems necessary to duplicate resources used previous to an unplanned interruption. The recovery of all resources will happen most effectively when a resources recovery element is included in an interruption reaction plan. A recovery plan should include a list of resources needed to resume operations and a list of places where those necessary resources can be found.

The reaction plan should include plans and procedures for initial response to an upset condition, plans and procedures for resumption of an effective level of business operations, and plans and procedures for the recovery of all resources needed to resume operations. Having these elements in place and implemented will set the stage for full restoration of normal business or other operations. Full restoration of normal operations means returning to or exceeding a level of operational effectiveness that existed before an unplanned interruption occurred. Achieving full restoration of normal operations is really the objective of a well-developed interruption reaction plan.

To recap, effective creation of the **reaction** component to be included in a business continuity plan should involve:

➡ A plan that assures an appropriate and immediate response to a business interruption.

➡ A plan that assures an effective and immediate resumption of a meaningful level of normal business operations.

➡ A plan that assures full recovery of resources needed to continue business operations.

➡ A plan that enables the full restoration of operations and accomplishes that at a similar or higher level of effectiveness than was being experienced before an unplanned interruption of normal business operations.

## *Summary*

The development of a well-conceived business continuity plan should contain three components. The ***preparation component*** should include appropriate actions that initiate the business continuity planning process, a careful and thoughtful risk evaluation, and a business impact analysis used to identify and quantify potential risks along with determining the potential impact of those risks. Additionally, the preparation plan should include the development of organization-wide business continuity strategies and communication of those risks, costs, and strategies to appropriate personnel that must be involved in the planning and implementation process.

Following the steps taken above, a business continuity plan should be developed and documented. Training programs should be developed and used to train the personnel involved with business continuity responsibilities. Finally, a plan should be frequently tested and exercised in efforts to assure that it is current, responsive, effective, efficient, and meets all business continuity objectives of the organization.

The **prevention component** of the business continuity plan should include prevention policies and appropriately created standards applied for purchase and use of equipment, computers and peripherals, telecommunication networks, processes, procedures, and other systems employed in operating the business. The prevention plan should also include operating, process, and procedure application guidelines that assure consistent utilization of standards and guidelines. IT and general computer architectures should also be carefully designed to avoid incompatibility between systems and networks.

When the above steps are completed, the prevention plan should be developed, documented, communicated to stakeholders, and implemented. A change management element should be included as part of continual efforts to assure the plan is updated as changes require. Again, it is important for the prevention plan to be monitored on a continuing basis and appropriate steps taken to assure ongoing compliance with requirements of the interruption prevention plan.

The **reaction component** of the plan outlines an organization's reaction procedures to be used in the event of an unplanned interruption of normal business or other operations. The reaction component should include procedures designed to assure effective emergency response, successful resumption of an acceptable level of operation, and procedures necessary for recovery of information, systems, telecommunication networks, and other resources needed to get back to full operation. The ultimate objective of a reaction plan is to restore full and normal business operations as quickly, efficiently, and effectively as possible.

All three of the components described above must be integrated into a single documented and deployable business continuity plan. All components and their elements must be carefully, thoughtfully, and thoroughly developed; communicated to appropriate responsible personnel; documented in an effective format and media (paper, three ring binder, computerized database, etc.); deployed; monitored for compliance; tested and exercised frequently; and updated as operating processes change.

And, do not forget to protect the completed business continuity plan itself. Safeguard the plan by having a copy or copies protected in more than one off-site location. Establish a protocol for access to the plan by limiting access to those responsible personnel who need to know how, where, and when to execute the plan. Limit access to those who know how to apply their actions to combine with the actions of others and to minimize or eliminate opportunities for sabotaging the steps included in an effective business continuity plan.

Develop the plan, communicate it, implement it, integrate it, monitor it, test and exercise it, execute it when necessary, change it when required, and protect it carefully. Remember that an effective business continuity plan will serve as a valuable resource for effectively protecting an organization's facilities, information, processes, markets, and employees. Also, in a global and unpredictable marketplace, full protection of all assets, including those mentioned above, can provide a real, strategic, and strong competitive advantage. Protection of valuable assets is worth spending an appropriate amount of money for what in true reality becomes "business continuity insurance" and the source of much managerial peace of mind.

# Chapter 13

## ROLES OF SUPPLIERS IN HIGH-PERFORMANCE FACILITIES MANAGEMENT

### *Value Your Suppliers and Make Them Members of Your Team*

"Suppliers" are those individuals, groups, and organizations that invent, develop, produce, and deliver products and services that enable high-quality work and personal lives. They are often also referred to as "vendors". It is extremely important that facilities managers and supplier representatives have mutually respectful and trusting relationships so they can combine their thinking, creativity, knowledge, and efforts to collectively address and resolve workplace management issues.

Suppliers' representatives should be and usually are solvers of problems whose efforts result in creating and providing appropriate solutions for meeting their client and customer needs. Suppliers can be viewed as essential lifelines that combine to assure that many needed resources will be available to enable totally integrated workplace development and management. Their success is always highly dependent upon them knowing their systems, products, and services as well as knowing what their competitors' systems, products, and services can or cannot do.

Professional suppliers' representatives become key individuals in assisting facilities managers and their other clients and customers to analyze available systems, products, and services alternatives and to select those that will have the highest probability of being successful solutions. Supplier representatives will obviously have biases toward systems, products, and services they represent and logically biases against competitors' offerings. However, their analyses of competitors' systems, products, and services should prompt astute facilities managers to fully investigate those biases and factor the results of those investigations into product and services acquisition decisions.

Many facilities managers, like other professionals, evolve almost a love-hate relationship with some supplier organizations and supplier representatives. Many facilities managers learn to love suppliers because they usually assist in solving problems. Supplier representatives can provide current-to-the-moment information about systems and products that have potential to address user problems. And, they usually can be great sources of education and training relative to their areas of specialization and about the systems, products, and services they represent.

Supplier representatives usually know how to apply their systems, products, and services to meet client and customer requirements. Supplier representatives are often well-schooled in SWOT analysis (strengths, weaknesses, opportunities, and threats). SWOT analysis typically involves suppliers' analyses of a situation and presentations of their systems, products, and services strengths, weaknesses, opportunities, and threats as potentially applied to defined client and customer needs. When supplier representatives perform thoughtful and in-depth SWOT analyses, they will have taken valuable steps toward understanding client or customer requirements. They then typically can identify ways to address those requirements, design and provide solutions that meet those requirements, and then provide ongoing service and support of those solutions.

Why would some facilities managers and other clients and customers sometimes become frustrated with supplier representatives? Supplier representatives can use up a lot of your valuable time. If they call on you too often for trivial reasons, they can become a nuisance. If their integrity has been compromised or their ethics are not at high levels, they can be downright dangerous sources of information or recommendations that ultimately prove to be just plain wrong. Eventually, they may get a lot of your money, too!

## Qualities of the Best Supplier Organizations and Representatives

**The great supplier organizations** are historically those that offer the highest quality state-of-the-art products and services. The great ones endeavor to provide those systems, products, and services that are regarded broadly as among the best in their industry. The great supplier organizations also develop and maintain reputations as providers of consistently responsive and high-quality customer-oriented organization-to-organization and person-to-person service.

**The great supplier organizations** fill their staffs with truly professional supplier representatives. They employ mature individuals with com-

184

prehensive and current-to-the-moment industry knowledge and with current-to-the-moment systems and products knowledge. They help those representatives develop analytical abilities to determine client and customer needs and to plan solutions to meet those needs. And, the great supplier organizations employ representatives with excellent personal qualities enabling them to work effectively with people on a continuing basis. Finally, the great supplier organizations employ representatives who have commitments to the golden rule and who maintain high levels of honesty, ethics, and integrity.

*The great supplier representatives* are, first and foremost, high-quality people. They are people you want to look up to and admire, the kind of people you know you can trust, and people who always tell the truth. They are people who genuinely want to get to know you as individuals and as customers, and they are the kind of people with whom you enjoy being associated.

Professionally and technically, the great supplier representatives become increasingly adept and successful at assisting clients and customers to identify and understand opportunities for improvement or for updating existing situations. The great ones develop high-level abilities to sift and sort out symptoms from real problems.

The great ones will function in intermediary roles between and among manufacturers and clients or customers. They will help clients and customers get appropriate pricing. They will expedite ordering and procurement, refine contracts, and expedite shipments. The great ones will work to coordinate deliveries and setups, creatively provide or coordinate needed training, work together to meet other needs, and provide follow-up services after sales or provision of services.

*Ultimately, the great supplier representatives* will be able to recommend appropriate and correct solutions—whether those solutions are their own systems, products, and services or theirs combined with systems, products, and services from other suppliers. Finally, the great ones will not be afraid to admit, in those situations where systems, products, or services from their organization may not fit immediate needs or provide total solutions, that clients or customers may need to collaborate with other suppliers for assistance.

# Engaging and Involving Supplier Organizations and Representatives

It is hard to play with other players if they are on another playing field, court, or sheet of ice. Teamwork happens not only when teams are formed but when individual team members come together and decide to work together to achieve common goals and objectives. So it is when it comes to maximizing the expertise of supplier organizations and their representatives. Finding them (or giving them opportunities to find you) is an important part of the process. Facilities managers' responsibilities—major responsibilities—include identifying and finding resources (including supplier organizations and supplier representatives) that have obvious potential for being of assistance.

What are often successful ways to find quality supplier organizations and supplier representatives? Facilities managers and others seeking high-quality supplier organizations and representatives should go into the identification and selection process with the understanding that carefully selecting suppliers will have both immediate and long-term impact on their programs and organizations.

As a rule of thumb, look locally first. Determine which supplier organizations and representatives have excellent reputations for providing quality systems, products, and services within your immediate geographic area. There should be several premiums and values on being good neighbors and shopping in your own neighborhood. Use the Internet and join professional associations and local chapters of those associations where you will often meet and become acquainted with supplier representatives. Attend trade shows where suppliers are exhibiting their products and presenting their services. Do not forget to use sources as fundamental as the yellow pages of your phone directory. Check with national, regional, and local chambers of commerce.

There are a number of ways consumers can go about performing background checks, and among those methods are having a Dunn & Bradstreet profile generated. Methodically check with local Better Business Bureaus, both to identify potential suppliers as well as to learn about them. Build and maintain awareness of supplier reputations through continual participation in area business tradeshows and expositions. Aggressively network locally and nationally for purposes of zeroing in on those supplier organizations and representatives that would appear to have high probabilities of meeting your organizations' immediate and long-term needs.

186

Professionalism; reputation; evidence of staying power; and continuing commitments to providing current and state-of-the-art systems, products, and services are essential. Having a history of employing high-quality, well educated, and industry-experienced personnel who collectively have shown consistent track records of operating ethically in all that they do is also essential. Finding them, checking them out, getting to know them, and treating them as business partners will be so important to maintaining strong supplier organization and strong supplier representative relationships over extended periods of time.

Do not overlook many potential suppliers who may be right under your nose at the present time. Recognize them. Supplier representatives could be a receptionist at the front door, salespersons, installers of products, or technical personnel who repair and maintain systems and facilities. They might include manufacturer representatives, consultants, systems integrator companies, VADs (value-added dealers), VARs (value-added resellers), and clerks at local retail or wholesaler outlets. The point is that product representatives take many shapes and forms, but all may be viable potential suppliers.

There will be multiple positive benefits to facilities managers from involving supplier representatives at varying levels as part of your facilities management teams. Include them on your teams early in the process of project definition and development. As early participants, supplier representatives will have exposure to issues and objectives associated with specific projects. Based on their early and comprehensive understanding of project objectives, they will usually be considerably more capable of assisting with the development of systems, products, and services that may serve as appropriate solutions to organizational needs. Supplier organizations and supplier representatives are valuable potential partners for facilities managers and can collectively work toward the development and management of totally integrated workplaces.

## *Manage Supplier Relationships Appropriately*

Historically, there have been periods of time and many places around the world where organizations went about doing their business routinely using tactics involving questionable ethics. The tactics that today may be questionable may have been normal parts of doing business in some places and some times in days gone by. Historically, it has not been unusual for supplier organizations to willingly offer friendly companions, luxury vacations, free products, tickets to entertainment events, meals, and many other incentives to potential purchasers as inducements to gain sales and business. While these incentives are not always inappropriate, there must be a continuing awareness that the ramifications of accepting such purchasing incentives may place purchasers in situations where their objectivity and integrity can then be questioned.

The importance of managing supplier relationships professionally, caringly, and in very straight-forward ways cannot be overemphasized. The news media today is often loaded with examples of questionable business practices. In cases where those questionable practices have been investigated, analyzed, and sometimes prosecuted, the resultant damage to organizational and individual reputations has been huge. Some things are just not worth the risk. Facilities managers and other potential purchasers of systems, products, and services must always remain committed to consistently high standards of ethical behavior.

## *Summary*

Supplier organizations and supplier representatives can play many important roles for and with facilities managers in the successful development and management of totally integrated workplaces. Supplier organizations and supplier representatives should be valued and included as members of facilities management teams. There are great supplier organizations and great supplier representatives that can combine to be incredibly powerful resources for and allies to professional facilities managers. Engaging and involving reputable supplier organizations and representatives always need to be done appropriately and ethically.

# Chapter 14
## MANAGING AND MOTIVATING
## FACILITIES MANAGEMENT PERSONNEL

### *Managing and Motivating Toward Productivity and Excellence*

One of the most important and challenging responsibilities of facilities managers is the successful management of their employees and staff. Facilities managers work with many resources to meet workplace development and management needs of organizations. Of all those resources, people—the human resources—are the most expensive and important.

Most facilities managers spend more time managing and working with people than they spend planning, developing, and managing facilities. People are expensive, their productivity or lack thereof is critical to program successes or failures, and their individual and collective approaches to their work determines in large part whether workplaces will be positive and satisfying or negative and unproductive.

Facilities managers who are or who aspire to be responsible for other people's work must grapple with the intricacies of human motivation. Whether it is within a family, in schools, on athletic teams, in small or large government agencies, in small businesses, within major corporations, or within association groups, high levels of motivation are so important. Anyone responsible for overseeing the work of others can benefit in many ways from developing an understanding of what motivating people toward excellence and productivity is all about.

We are all living and working in an era when there are occasional conflicts between the often dehumanizing effects of technologies and the deep needs expressed by people in our workforce. These needs for recognition of their own individual wants, desires to receive intrinsic satisfaction from their work, longing for respect and responsiveness, and needs for job challenges all impact on their approaches to their work lives.

We are also living and managing in times when our personnel are members of an affluent society. Employees today have higher expectations for their careers in terms of responsibility, advancement, compensation, and status. People want more today, they are likely to want even more in the future, and they continue to want it faster and faster.

People today want and expect more openness, more involvement, and expect more input into decision-making processes. And, they see these as entitlements—not just something to be earned over many years of service. People want to feel good about themselves and will be productive and strive for excellence if they do. If they do not feel good about themselves, there will be a tendency toward poor performance and often they will also keep others from doing their best.

## Facilities and Technology Are Not Enough... You Need Motivated People!

Facilities managers can now have architecturally fantastic facilities and an amazing array of tried-and-proven technologies available for use in developing and augmenting organization-wide facilities management programs. CAD systems for facilities development and modification, the Internet, intranets, computer-based facilities monitoring and management systems, facilities management websites, and other technologies that make possible the development of high-quality facilities and systems. Now, facilities managers have more great options than ever before for achieving high-performance facilities management.

Great facilities and state-of-the-art technologies alone, however, will not be enough for success. You need motivated people! You may have the finest facilities and technology systems available. However, if your personnel who are to be the supervisors, employees, and users on a day-in and day-out basis are not satisfied with their jobs and roles and are not motivated toward productivity and excellence, then the potential of your technology systems are unlikely to be fully realized. Remember the adage that it is not the facilities and tools that people use, it is how the people who use those facilities and tools go about using them that leads either to success or to unfortunate results.

## Be Sensitive to the Human Dimension

Motivation in facilities management is, first of all, a matter of human understanding. It requires managers knowing their personnel and understanding what is and is not important to them. That understanding requires more effort today than ever before and will require even greater

190

efforts in our new millennium.  Many aspects of workplaces and of work-forces are changing.  In an era of war on terrorism; corporate downsizing, rightsizing, restructuring, merging, and splitting up; and accelerated paces of change; people tend to be less sure about their jobs, roles, responsibil-ities, security, and their futures.

Along with continued changes in workplaces and in workforces have also come continually changing employee values. Today, employees and personnel at all levels are increasingly expressing needs for recognition, job challenge, and achievement.  More people in the workforce are better edu-cated and recognition by their leaders, opportunities to participate in man-agement decisions, and having feelings that their work is useful and contributing to the common good are sometimes more important than salary and benefits.

People want workplaces and environments where they can develop good self-concepts.  Good self-concepts are like security blankets in that if you have a good one, things bother you much less and there is less likelihood there will be vulnerabilities to insecurities, fears, and problems.  People know that if they can place a high value on themselves, then others are likely to do the same.  People want to have work situations in which they can achieve, and they want to be understood, appreciated, and respected. Remembering that valuable formula in any kind of organizational work is so important to motivating people and to then achieving results through those motivated people.

Historically, those managers and leaders who are not especially sensi-tive to the human dimension and who make managerial or technical deci-sions which ignore basic human needs, habits, abilities, and wants often see their actions leading to lower productivity, alienation, sabotage, turnover, and other unfortunate results.  It may well be that one of the greatest unsatisfied needs today is to be loved, wanted, and appreciated.

Examine your own feelings and answer this question.  Have you had too much love, appreciation, feelings of positive reinforcement, and self worth? If you are like most people, you could probably use more of each.  This means that when you give other people—including your employees and personnel—sincere compliments, words of appreciation, gentle words of encouragement, and challenges to greatness, they will almost always be gratefully received.  Understand those aspects of the human dimension and strive to fill those needs for people, and you are likely to experience success as a manager and leader.

## The Managers' and Leaders' Challenge

Present and future participative managers and leaders must contribute to the evolution of work environments where employees and personnel can fully achieve group goals with the least amount of resources and with the greatest amount of personnel satisfaction. And, it may be said that the most successful managers and leaders almost always have two critically important characteristics—they are going somewhere and they are able to persuade other people to go with them.

The most successful managers and leaders are usually those who recognize and internalize that they have an inescapable social responsibility for the effects of their thoughts, words, and deeds upon the lives of others. They think about the consequences of their thoughts, words, and deeds before they say or do them. They believe deeply that people are precious and important, and they recognize that their impact for good on the lives of others is essential to their success in getting results through people.

## What Really is Motivation?

Motivation may be defined or explained in many ways. Motivation is an internal process that causes people to take some particular action because they want to take that action. On the surface, that is very basic. To motivate people, the encyclopedias and other books tell us, is to cause them to act in certain ways. That is accomplished by furnishing them with motives to do what they are being asked to do. Children usually learn that being bad in the eyes of their parents may result in scoldings while being good often earns rewards of some type. In other words, those parents have instilled in their children the dual motive of avoiding punishment and earning rewards.

In professional management, the system of reward and punishment has been described as a carrot-and-stick approach—a carrot being dangled in front of a donkey's nose or a stick being applied to the hindquarters. In this fashion, the donkey is alternately enticed or impelled toward a master's goals. Whether the donkey ever gets to eat the carrot is usually not made very clear in management literature, however we can be quite sure that it often gets to feel the stick.

Workers today, from entry-level employees to members of top management, are clearly motivated by much more than the carrot of pay and advancement or the stick of insecurity and discipline although those factors do continue to be very important. Complex and not always easy-to-understand motives influence today's and tomorrow's women and men in the workforce. Money might not be everything, but most people continue to have a strong desire for the comfort and possessions that money will purchase. And, it is part of normal human nature to avoid the stick, stay clear of trouble, and to want the assurances and security of steady, well-paid jobs.

It is clear that the function of motivation in modern management is to create the appropriate environment and influence employees to perform to the best of their abilities. Accomplishing this objective requires knowledgeable and conscientious managers who concentrate on creating and maintaining psychological climates which cause and enable people to want to do their very best. While there are many theories about how to get people to drive themselves, no one disputes the fundamental notion that high-level motivation resulting in high-level performance must come from within individuals themselves.

## *The Hierarchy of Needs*

Abraham Maslow suggested in his classic book *Motivation and Personality* (New York: Harper & Row Publishers, Inc., 1954) that people are motivated by their desire to satisfy a set of five universal needs: (1) basic physiological needs, (2) safety and security needs, (3) belonging and social needs, (4) esteem and status needs, and (5) self-actualization or self-realization needs. Those needs are presented in hierarchical (pyramid) form with the basic needs at the bottom and self-actualization needs at the top. According to Maslow, each person is a wanting being and always has some need to be satisfied. Once that need is satisfied, however, it no longer motivates as individuals then seek the satisfaction of another—and usually higher-level—need.

Maslow further believed that people will satisfy their needs according to a particular order. Level 2 needs do not dominate until level 1 needs are reasonably satisfied. Level 3 needs do not dominate until Level 2 needs have been adequately met. This process continues until needs at the last level, Level 5, have been reached. But, the needs at this level are never completely satisfied. People strive to satisfy their lowest-order needs first (their basic survival needs). Higher-order needs do not become important until the basic needs have been adequately satisfied. Once the basic needs have been fulfilled, they will no longer motivate.

The first of these three categories are easy enough to understand. People naturally want the necessities of life. They want comfortable and secure working conditions and fair compensation. They want to feel that they belong to a group or groups of supportive people and to be a part of something successful that is bigger than they are as individuals.

However, the needs that come under the heading of need for identity are more difficult to understand. They involve a desire for recognition, status, and opportunities to demonstrate their competence. In many instances, these needs may not be readily apparent to an individual employee's supervisor—in this instance the facilities manager.

Employees' needs for self-actualization or self-realization may also be overlooked. These needs include having challenges to one's abilities, having opportunities to utilize creativity, and having a reasonable amount of personal autonomy—all needs that often can not be met completely within work environments even though it is known that they have strong effects on individuals' attitudes toward their jobs.

The results are that whether individual employees (and all employees collectively) care more about money than self-realization or more about self-expression and identity than creature comforts varies from individual to individual. And, the intensity of one need or another within an individual will vary according to circumstances—such as people becoming more preoccupied with security as they grow older.

## *What Do People Really Want From Their Jobs?*

Management and sociological researchers have investigated (in multiple studies within varied environments including blue-collar through white-collar personnel crossing age and cultural ranges) what do employees and personnel really want from their jobs. While investigating factors such as good working conditions, feeling included, tactful disciplining, full appreciation for work done, management loyalty to employees, good wages or salary, promotion and growth within organizations, job security, interesting work, and sympathetic understanding of personal problems, the results have all basically concluded that what employees and personnel want from their jobs are:

➡ Interesting and stimulating work;

➡ Appreciation for work that is done, and especially if done well;

194

→ Understanding of personal problems;

→ Feeling included; and

→ Good wages or salary.

Yes, money is very important—but it is most important when it comes along with having interesting and stimulating work, being appreciated, being loved, feeling wanted, being understood, feeling that one is not being left out, and other important factors. A major point to remember is that employees and personnel are clearly motivated by multiple, complex, and not always easy-to-understand factors and motives.

## Customized and Individualized Motivation is Required

All of this means that **any attempt to motivate a person to do her or his best work must always be customized to the needs of individual personalities.** Because of this extremely important fact, the person most responsible for an employee's motivation (next to the employee herself or himself) is her or his immediate supervisor. The top management of organizations can go quite a distance toward meeting security and creature comfort needs and in offering incentives for good performance. However, the more private and specific elements of motivation must be on a personal level between a manager and an employee on a day-to-day basis, over a period of time.

Some managers, including facilities managers, have not recognized the special importance of their roles in motivational processes and of how managers' actions can help or hinder. Many managers make the mistake of believing that other parts of their work are more pressing or important. But it is a fact that these managers cannot escape the influence of motivation or of its opposite—demotivation. **The motivation of each individual in a group is what combines to make up a group's morale.** Great morale will always be an incredibly valuable asset while bad morale will work against managers and leaders in any situation or organization.

The results from surveys of employee attitudes in recent years emphasize the importance of motivation at the ground level and on up. Surveys reinforce that today's employees place a strong emphasis on challenge, opportunity, and recognition of performance. And, the surveys report that people are way more willing than their counterparts of a generation ago to quit a job that does not offer these components.

Facilities managers who fail to thoughtfully and consistently consider employees' individual and collective priorities may have to live with the consequences. These consequences usually consist of high turnover, its consequent costs, having to function with apathetic staff, or working with disgruntled staff. Managers, on the other hand, who make serious efforts to understand their employees usually are much more successful and usually become better motivated themselves in that they often come closer to meeting their own self-esteem and self-actualization needs in the process.

## What are the Characteristics of Effective Work Groups?

Formal research has been conducted and veteran managers have been surveyed relative to what they believe are characteristics of effective work groups. Results show that those managers who are genuinely interested in fostering good human relations and in developing intrinsically-motivated personnel strive for work environments which include:

- ***Mutual support*** with group members having genuine concerns for each others' job welfare, growth, and personal success;
- ***Mutual trust*** in which each member of groups feel free to express opinions, express feelings about issues, ask questions, or disagree with the positions of others without concern for retaliation, ridicule, or negative consequences;
- ***Genuine communication*** in which members of groups are open and where there is not concern about games being played behind peoples' backs;
- ***Accepting conflicts as normal*** and working them through, recognizing that it is from positive conflict resolution that most growth and innovation are derived; and
- ***Mutual respect for individual differences*** which allows for delegation from manager to employees, from leader to members, employees to employees, members to members, and sometimes even employees to manager or members to leaders.

Historically, when these characteristics of effective work groups exist, the whole (the group) becomes greater than the sum of its individual parts. A much greater likelihood exists that the motivation of each of the individuals and the morale of entire groups will be positive and high. A great source of energy for people is that of having pride in the work they are doing, pride in their organizations, and pride in their co-workers and associates with whom they are privileged to work. Compatible relationships with meaningful people combine to create climates of organizational effectiveness in which people are likely to be highly motivated.

## Principles for Managing and Motivating Facilities Management Personnel

Facilities managers can learn to increase their effectiveness in motivating and managing personnel. Consider implementing and following several important principles and approaches for managing and working effectively with people in technologically-intensive work environments:

➥ **Develop clear lines of authority and responsibility.** Develop organizational charts and straightforward online employee manuals for use in describing your organization to current or potential employees. Job applicants as well as current employees want and deserve to know where their departments or units and where their own jobs and responsibilities fit into organizations. Be ready to show them and live by it.

➥ **Be sure that each person understands the organizational structure and knows who is responsible to whom.** Take steps to ensure that each current employee and potential employees understand the general structure of the organization as a whole and specifically understand the organizational structure of their division, department, or unit. Who reports to whom should be very clear to all personnel. People want to know, individually and collectively, where they fit in organizations in relation to others. Help them learn quickly and understand thoroughly, and you will be highly regarded by them as a result.

➥ **No member of organizations should report to more than one supervisor.** A tremendously important principle of management with origins in the Bible is the fundamental principle that it is difficult, if not impossible, for one individual to serve more than one master. Take steps to ensure that each employee will be responsible to only one immediate supervisor or manager—at least for any one project. Today's extensive use of teams and matrix organizations seems to stretch this principle, but it remains extremely important.

➡ ***Assign all necessary functions and strive to achieve a fair distribution of work.*** In all work groups, teams, or units, it is important that all the work gets done that is supposed to be done. Accomplish this objective by using periodic staff meetings to review your group's total responsibilities and to determine which of your staff members will be primarily responsible for each of the various jobs to be done. In that process, strive to achieve an equitable and fair distribution of work. People will generally work hard and work enthusiastically if they know that work to be accomplished is appropriately divided and if they are confident they will be appropriately recognized for the work they do.

➡ ***Authority and responsibility must go hand in hand.*** Do not give someone a job to do (responsibility for the performance of work) unless you are also willing to give them the authority (the right to make and implement decisions and the right to command) necessary to do the job. Effective delegation is often one of the most difficult aspects of managing for new managers to learn. Either delegate authority commensurate with responsibility, or do not delegate at all.

➡ ***Carefully evaluate the span of control in your organization.*** The span of control refers to the number of people who can be effectively and comfortably managed by one manager. That number varies with every situation and there is no optimum number. It is important for all managers that the scope of their responsibilities is not so small and narrow that they are bored and unchallenged. And, it is equally important that their jobs and the scope of their work is not so great that they are spread too thin to be effective. Periodically evaluate the appropriateness of your own span of control in your current managerial situation.

➡ ***Authority and responsibility for work to be done should be decentralized to persons responsible for doing that work.*** The person who knows a job the best is usually the person who does that job. Keeping that adage in mind, it is important that managers delegate work to those members of their staffs who usually do the type of work in question. The result will usually be work that is done knowledgeably and effectively and also is accomplished at the lowest costs to organizations.

➡ **Consider implementing the concept of "management by exception."** The primary responsibilities of managers are to plan, organize, staff, direct, and control operations—not to spend excessive amounts of time overseeing routine activities. The most able and successful managers delegate thoroughly and effectively so that substantial portions of their time is reserved for planning and further development.

➡ **Policies and operating procedures should be developed and distributed.** Develop facilities management procedural manuals and have them available on a website. Simply stated, every organization needs a facilities management manual if high-quality organization-wide facilities management programs are to be operated and managed successfully on an on-going basis.

➡ **Provide orientation and periodic training for all categories of personnel.** Many experienced facilities managers, other veteran managers, and management researchers agree that time spent orienting and training personnel is returned up to ten times annually in terms of time saved by not having to deal with problems caused by failures to orient and train. A common characteristic of the most successful managers is that they almost all make high priorities of providing high-quality initial orientation and continual on-going staff training and development.

➡ **Provide for continual follow up and appraisal of work performance.** Every system will benefit from systematic follow-up. Football and basketball coaches have their games and often their practices videotaped or otherwise recorded. University professors administer periodic examinations. Physicians frequently require re-examination following surgery, therapy, or administration of medications. Follow-up activities in offices may be subjective, such as periodic staff discussions of various work activities and the strengths and weaknesses of present approaches to accomplishing that work. Or, the follow-up may be very specific and involve the use of quantitative approaches such as counting facilities maintenance processes, repair events attempted and made, or other quantifiable facilities operations within organizations. Be creative, and take steps to develop appropriate approaches for the follow up of work activities.

➡ ***Consider centralizing managerial control over major functions.*** Centralized managerial control does not mean that all of the work involved with specific functions needs to be physically centralized. Even though most organizations have physically decentralized buildings, other facilities, and systems throughout their divisions, departments, and units, it is highly desirable to centralize management control over facilities management functions and to have one individual in place as the organization's facilities manager.

➡ ***Remember that all organizations are comprised of several functions that must work well independently but that are interrelated and must work well together.*** The systems view of organizations stresses that the parts of organizations must each function well if entire organizations are to function efficiently and well as wholes. Successful managers plan for the overall operation of their organizations and also strive to assure that each of the various subsystems or parts of organizations function well. In facilities management, partnering with all of the facilities stakeholders discussed in this book will be critical to the achievement of high-performance facilities management programs.

➡ ***Remember that your people are your most important and most valuable resource.*** The most valuable asset of any organization is its people and what those people know and can do. Successful facilities managers will benefit from focusing a majority of their attention, effort, and time on being successful in interacting with people. It is readily possible for individuals to develop into very effective motivators and very successful managers. New and veteran managers alike are encouraged to become continuing students of human behavior and to make their continuing development as people-oriented successful managers a major goal.

# Qualities of the Most Effective Facilities Managers, Motivators, and Leaders

What are the qualities of the most effective facilities managers, motivators, and leaders? Extensive surveys have been conducted in many work environments. Graduate students have made the topic one of very extensive research. Professional conventions and seminars have been created to focus on the question. Facilities managers and other managers continue to wrestle with the topic and its challenges on a day-in and day-out basis. The results of this formal investigation and informal consideration suggest that the qualities of the most effective facilities managers, motivators, and leaders include:

➡ ***Their integrity is above question.*** They live by the Golden Rule. They act ethically and morally in a sometimes seemingly unethical world.

➡ ***They are leaders.*** They are able to draw forth willing efforts from people and cause them to want to do their best rather than being dictators who try to force unwilling efforts out of people through use of power. They know that a person is no bigger than the way she or he treats other people.

➡ ***They are other-oriented and not selfish.*** Other people are always equally, if not the most important.

➡ ***They know the fundamentals of their discipline.*** The great facilities managers know the discipline of professional facilities management inside and out. They know their profession well.

➡ ***They treat each employee as an individual.*** The great ones value good personal relationships and they foster and provide personal recognition for their people.

➡ ***They recognize individual differences.*** They strive to diagnose specific situations and modify their managerial behavior accordingly. They know that any attempt to motivate a person to do her or his best must be tailor made to the needs of individual personalities. They get to know their people one by one by one.

- **They have a strong belief in human rights.** The great ones respect the rights of women, the rights of men, and the rights of everyone. They respect the dignity of people.

- **They are good listeners.** They treat people as persons and not as mere numbers, and they listen to people very carefully and intently.

- **They make decisions.** A distinguishing characteristic of great facilities managers is their ability to identify alternatives, appropriately evaluate options, and make decisions. They are not "wishy-washy." The great ones develop and use well-thought-out decision-making processes. In baseball umpiring terms, they will make the call when it is theirs to make.

- **They delegate.** The great facilities managers and other managers delegate consistently, appropriately, and encourage their employees to take on as much responsibility as they feel comfortable accepting.

- **They welcome suggestions for change.** The great ones promote climates in which employees are encouraged to be innovative, to examine existing procedures and practices, and to experiment with new solutions.

- **They encourage self-development of their personnel.** They always make orientation, education, and training high priorities. And, the great facilities managers develop personal programs for continuing education that they follow in order to keep learning themselves. They recognize that the great ones in any discipline stay current within their professions.

- **They give praise and credit when praise and credit are due.** The great ones acknowledge that recognition for jobs well done reinforces individuals' self-images and self-satisfaction and increases desires to make greater contributions to organizations in the future.

- **They are highly creative.** The great facilities managers routinely explore new concepts, develop new ideas, try new technologies, and are always looking for new ways to work effectively with people to get things done.

202

➥ **They are self confident.** The great ones have healthy attitudes about themselves and their circumstances. They know that their attitude, not just their aptitude, will be major factors in their successes.

➥ **They are happy people themselves and have good senses of humor.** The great ones do not take themselves too seriously and they are open and allow their personnel to get to know them as individuals.

➥ **They are highly motivated themselves.** The great facilities managers know it is virtually impossible to motivate others until you have learned to motivate yourself.

➥ **They work hard.** The great ones extend themselves, make the extra effort, go 150 percent, run the extra mile, and are determined self-starters. They lead by example.

➥ **They are optimistic, positive, and enthusiastic.** Very high percentages of the great facilities managers (and the great ones in any profession) are very optimistic people who are also consistently very positive. They typically display a contagious enthusiasm that rubs off on people around them. Instead of seeking blame in those few instances where something does not go as planned, they look for solutions.

➥ **They treat others as they themselves expect to be treated.** The great facilities managers do unto others as they would have others do unto them.

➥ **They look for the potential in people, and they go out of their ways to say "thanks."** The great ones send thank-you e-mail messages, make phone calls, leave voice-mail messages, write notes, and send cards that essentially say "Thank you—I appreciate you and who you are and what you do."

➥ **They have a deep personal faith.** The vast majority of the great ones believe deeply in a power much greater than themselves. For most, that deep faith is the basis for their living by the Golden Rule.

➥ **They care and care deeply.** The great facilities managers remember that everybody hurts from time to time, and that some hurt much more than others. So, they are sensitive to the needs and feelings of others. They know that some extremely powerful words are "May I help you" and "I really care about you and your situation." The great ones are supportive during difficult times.

## Summary

It is true that the most successful facilities managers are almost always those who pay the most attention to the people who work with them, work for them, and that follow them. Motivation is really not much different from friendship. It is treating people with respect for their individuality and having deep and genuine concerns for their feelings and needs.

Motivation is caring about people and giving them opportunities to show what they can do. Motivation means encouraging people and helping them to meet their full potential in their careers and in their lives. Above all, a friend is someone who will go out of her or his way to do things for you with the motive being nothing more than the knowledge that you would do the same for her or him.

And, so it is with management, motivation, and leadership in facilities management. The managers who are most concerned about their employees and the people around them usually get the most out of them in the form of high-quality performance. Those who are the most successful facilities managers, motivators, and leaders know they can no longer rely on older approaches or incentives to motivate today's and tomorrow's employees and personnel. In times of transition and change, management by authority must give way to people-oriented and caring professional management by objectives, teamwork, and custom-made motivation.

The most successful facilities managers are almost always those who genuinely care about their people. They appreciate their people and they express that appreciation in many ways. They say "thanks" genuinely, regularly, and consistently. They recognize that they still can learn more and become even more effective in interacting and working with other people. The great facilities management professionals know they can continue to develop their abilities to successfully manage and motivate facilities management and other personnel.

# Chapter 15
*RESOURCES FOR FACILITIES MANAGERS*

## Great Resources are Now Available About Facilities Management

The facilities management profession continues to evolve into a more and more sophisticated management discipline. As the costs associated with all aspects of facilities management continue to increase and as the global economy creates stronger and stronger competition among organizations, the need to intelligently manage all forms of assets has grown to be more critical than ever before in the history of commerce. Fortunately, there is a steadily increasing array of excellent resources now available to help facilities management stakeholders gather and use the intelligence they need in order to effectively develop and manage facilities. Facilities are among the most expensive assets owned by businesses, agencies, institutions, and organizations of all types. Knowledge resources provide the basis for accomplishing consistently successful integrated workplace development and management.

Literally thousands of resources now available relate directly to the challenges associated with management of built environments. University degree programs in facilities management, professional associations, publications, results of formal research, suppliers of products, and designers of buildings are among the many resources facilities managers can use to advance their knowledge and apply it to total workplace design and management. Collectively these resources relate to architecture, engineering, design, construction, furnishings and finishes, occupancy, maintenance, ongoing management, and all aspects of developing and managing places where people work and where commerce is conducted.

The resources about and related to facilities management presented in this chapter are first and foremost a "partial list" from among the vast number of resources that could be listed and recommended. Presented in random order, there is no intent by the authors to promote or fail to promote any college or university, organization, system, service, or product that may be of value and interest to facilities managers and facilities management stakeholders. Rather, it is the intent to provide an awareness of and means to access a "starter list" of those resources that the authors believe are especially relevant to facilities managers and the facilities management profession.

## University Degree Programs

The International Facility Management Association has developed standards to recognize high-quality facility management degree programs within colleges and universities. The recognized program initiative was designed to acknowledge and encourage the strengthening of state-of-the-art facility management degree programs. The following colleges and universities offer academic degrees in facility management. They qualified for recognition by submitting a detailed self-study application to IFMA that was reviewed and approved by a committee of peers.

These institutions re-apply for recognition every six years to ensure that the programs they offer continue to meet the standards set by IFMA for high-quality facility management education. The primary purpose for which the co-authors of this book provide this list is so that facilities managers, facilities management stakeholders, potential students, employers, and others with an interest in facility management education know which programs have been set apart by taking the steps needed to become recognized.

**Brigham Young University**
Provo, Utah
B.S. degree in Facilities Management
Contact:  Dr. Jeffrey Campbell, Chair, Facilities Management
801-422-8758

**Colorado State University-Pueblo**
Pueblo, Colorado
B. S. degree in Facilities Management and Technology Studies
Contact:  Mike Hoots
719-549-2838

**Cornell University**
Ithaca, New York
B. S. degree in Facilities Management
M.S. degree in Facilities Management
Contact:  Dr. William Sims, CFM
607-255-1954

206

**Ferris State University**
Big Rapids, Michigan
B. S. degree in Facilities Management
Contact:  Diane Nagelkirk
231-591-2630

**FHS Kufstein Bildungsgmbh**
Kufstein, Austria
Magister (FH) for Facility Management
Contact:
Thomas Madritsch, FHS
43/ 5372/71819

**The Hong Kong Polytechnic University**
Hung Hom, Kowloon, Hong Kong, China
Graduate Program in Facility Management
Contact:  Dr. Danny Then
(852) 2766 4558


## *Professional Associations*

**International Facility Management Association (IFMA)**
1 E. Greenway Plaza, Suite 1100
Houston, TX  77046-0194
713-623-4362
www.ifma.com

**American Institute of Architects (AIA)**
1735 New York Avenue N. W.
Washington, DC  20006-5292
800-AIA-3837
202-626-7300
www.aia.org

**ARMA International (ARMA)**
13725 West 109th Street, Suite 101
Lenexa, KS  66215
800-422-2762
913-341-3808
www.arma.org

## American Society of Heating, Refrigerating, and Air Conditioning Engineers (ASHRAE)
1791 Tullie Circle N. E.
Atlanta, GA 30329
800-527-4723
404-636-8400
www.ashrae.com

## American Society of Interior Designers (ASID)
608 Massachusetts Avenue, N. E.
Washington, DC 20002-6006
202-546-3480
www.asid.org

## American Society for Testing and Materials (ASTM)
100 Bar Harbor Drive
West Conshohocken, PA 19428-2959
610-832-9585
www.astm.org

## British Institute of Facilities Management (BIFM)
67 High Street
Saffron Walden
Essex CBIO 1AA
United Kingdom
01799 508606
www.bifm.org.uk

## CoreNetGlobal
260 Peachtree Street N. W., Suite 1500
Atlanta, GA 30303
800-726-8111
www.corenetglobal.org

## Building Owners and Managers Association (BOMA)
1201 New York Avenue, N. W.
Washington, DC 0005, Suite 300
202-408-2662
www.boma.org

**Facility Management Association of Australia (FMA)**
Suite 203, 2nd Floor
60 Leicester Street
Carlton VICTORIA 3053
Australia
03 9347 5100
www.fma.com.au

**Facility Management Nederland (FMN)**
+31 35 694 35 03
www.fmn.vereniging.nl

**International Interior Design Association (IIDA)**
13-122 Merchandise Mart
Chicago, IL  60654-1104
888-799-4432
312-467-1950
www.iida.org

**Japan Facility Management Association (JFMA)**
Contact through IFMA

**National Council for Interior Design Qualification (NCIDQ)**
1200 18th Street N. W., Suite 101
Washington, DC 20036-2506
www.ncidq.org
202-721-0220

**PRISM International**
605 Benson Road, Suite B
Garner, NC  27529
800-336-9793
919-771-0657
www.prismintl.org

## Government Agencies
## Independent Organizations
## Other Sources

### Americans with Disabilities Act Accessibility Guidelines (ADAAG)
www.access-board.gov

### American National Standards Institute
(ANSI)
1819 L Street, NW
Washington, DC 20036
202-293-8020
www.ansi.org

### Buffalo Organization for Social and Technological Innovation (BOSTI)
BOSTI Associates
351 Woodward Avenue
Buffalo, NY 14214
716-837-7120
www.bosti.com

### Environmental Protection Agency (United States) (EPA)
Ariel Rios Building
1200 Pennsylvania Avenue, NW
Washington, DC 20460
202-272-0167
www.epa.gov

### Federal Emergency Management Agency (FEMA)
500 C Street, SW
Washington, DC 20472
202-566-1600
www.fema.gov

### Information Requirements Clearinghouse, Inc. (IRCH)
5600 South Quebec Street, Suite 250-C
Greenwood Village, CO 80111
303-721-7500
www.irch.com

**International Organization for Standardization (ISO)**
1 rue de Varembe, Case postale 56
CH-1211   Geneva 20, Switzerland
+41 22 749 01 11
www.iso.ch/iso.en

**National Institute for Occupational Safety and Health (NIOSH)**
Hubert H. Humphrey Building
200 Independence Avenue, SW
Washington, DC  20201
800-356-4674
513-533-8328
www.cdc.gov/niosh

**Occupational Safety and Health Administration (OSHA)**
200 Constitution Avenue, NW
Washington, DC  20210
800-321-6742
www.osha.gov

## *The Tremendous Potential of Supplier Resources*

Suppliers play multiple valuable roles in on-going facilities management within organizations. While all suppliers obviously have vested interests in that they want to have their products and services selected and used, high-quality suppliers also value opportunities to provide their expertise and to provide valuable consulting services for facilities management stakeholders.

High-quality suppliers know that "what goes around, comes around," and they know that if they provide valuable expertise as a part of their total services, the result will often be getting business that some who focused only on products would not have gotten. Facilities managers should take advantage of the supplier resources and expertise that are volunteered or otherwise provided by them and that are available for use in developing high-performance facilities management programs.

At the risk of forgetting any very valuable resources, the authors of this book have elected to not list specific supplier companies or individuals. Nevertheless, they strongly encourage readers and all facilities management stakeholders to seek out and rely regularly on the expertise and good counsel that is available because of meaningful supplier relationships that have been developed.

The authors encourage readers to go to the websites of organizations cited throughout this book and utilize and benefit from the systems, products, services, and expertise available from these high-quality sources. Leveraging the value of these websites can lead readers and other facilities management stakeholders to identifying, locating, and connecting with suppliers who may become extremely valuable partners.

## *IFMA Courses, Seminars, and the annual World Workplace Conference and Exposition*

The International Facility Management Association (IFMA) consistently offers a growing array of professional development courses, seminars, products, and services for individuals seeking to expand their facilities management knowledge. Whether individuals are preparing for certification, pursuing careers in facilities management, or simply seeking to improve their facilities management knowledge and skills, IFMA's Professional Development program offers many options and resources. Courses range from one-day, two-day, three-day, and five-day programs to ones of other lengths on topics including:

Introduction to Facility Management I:  The FM Profession
Introduction to Facility Management II:  Leading the FM Department
Introduction to Facility Management III:  Making Financial Decisions
Introduction to Facility Management IV:  Delivering FM Services
Introduction to Facility Management V:  Managing FM Information
The Financial Competency Course
The Leadership & Management Competency Course
The Operations & Maintenance Competency Course
The Real Estate Competency Course
The Planning & Project Management Competency Course
The Quality Assessment & Innovation Competency Course
The Communication Competency Course
The Human & Environmental Factors Competency Course
The Technology Competency Course
The CFM Exam Review

IFMA also periodically presents FM Edge Audio Seminars that typically present cutting-edge FM topics in 90-minute interactive teleconference format with an Internet-presentation option. Participants can gain current facilities management information from their homes, offices, or within groups at workplaces. Past FM Leading Edge Audio seminars are available on cassettes.

IFMA's annual World Workplace Conference & Expo provides excellent annual opportunities for facilities managers and other facilities management stakeholders to continue learning about the industry, share knowledge and experiences, and network with fellow professionals. Year after year, IFMA partners with other highly respected organizations in related industries to create countless networking and educational opportunities.

Companies exhibiting on the expo floor represent a diverse range of products and services. Exhibitors show and demonstrate state-of-the-art products and services now available for implementation and use. Annually the World Workplace Conference & Expo provides multiple opportunities for attendees to learn what is new in the industry, discuss latest trends, review new technologies and research, and examine new products and services. For more information about IFMA's annual World Workplace Conference & Expo, go to the association's website at www.worldworkplace.org.

## The IFMA Products and Services Catalog

IFMA is a member-centered organization that exists to guide and develop facilities management professionals. IFMA's vision is to serve as the ultimate resource and representative for facilities management. The association publishes an annual Products and Services Catalog which contains information about professional development offerings, IFMA chapters and councils, and about a steadily increasing array of IFMA Bookstore products and services. In addition to acquiring and utilizing the paper catalog, visit IFMA's electronic catalog on the association's website at www.ifma.org/store.

# The Facility Management Journal

The *Facility Management Journal* is a leading source of current, credible facilities management news for industry professionals. Published by IFMA, the *Facility Management Journal* is written specifically for professionals who are concerned with developing and managing totally integrated workplaces. The bimonthly *Facility Management Journal* is one of the benefits of IFMA membership and is also available by subscription to non-members of the association. The *Facility Management Journal* continues its reputation as one of the most respected resources for professionals seeking the knowledge that enables the development of high-performance facilities management programs.

# Glossary

**Architecture**

The art and science of developing plans for buildings and facilities. Architects typically focus on site selection, analysis and articulation of needs for facilities, design, oversight of construction, inspection and approval of construction processes, and related functions.

**ARMA International**

An international professional association for records management professionals throughout the United States, Canada, and 30 other countries (www.arma.org).

**Audit**

A thorough inspection designed to ultimately provide senior management, facilities managers, and others with data and information on which to base strategic planning.

**Benchmark**

A standard or point of reference for measuring or judging quality, value, and relevancy.

**Benchmarking**

Process of gathering operational data from peer-type organizations for purposes of comparison, judging quality, measuring value, developing best practices, and determining relevancy.

**Budget**

A collection of categories and accounting entries within which all ongoing (facilities) operational costs are identified, captured, analyzed, understood, and forecasted in relationship to organizational and (facilities) management operating objectives.

| | |
|---|---|
| **Building maintenance** | The upkeep of building components typically including HVAC (heating, ventilation, and air conditioning), electrical, elevators, carpentry, painting, and related components. |
| **Business continuity plan** | Specific plans by organizations for continuing and maintaining operations in the event of terrorism, disasters, or other upset conditions. |
| **CFM** | Certified Facility Manager, the international professional designation for facilities management professionals who attain necessary educational qualifications, possess necessary facilities management experience, and pass a qualifying examination. The CFM is a respected global credential in facilities management that sets the standard for ensuring the knowledge and abilities of practicing facilities managers. |
| **CRM** | Certified Records Manager, the international professional designation for records management professionals who attain necessary educational qualifications, possess necessary records management experience, and pass a six-part qualifying examination administered by the Institute of Certified Records Managers. |
| **CAD system** | A computer-based software system used for drawing construction plans, floor plans, space accounting, population inventory, furniture inventory, maintenance records, cost allocation, and other data used in the management of facilities management programs. |

216

| | |
|---|---|
| **Churn** | The total number of employee workplace moves made in a year divided by the total number of employees in that facility, multiplied by 100. |
| **Civil engineering** | A branch of professional engineering that typically focuses on the design of highways, bridges, tunnels, waterworks, harbors, and related structures. |
| **Code of ethics** | A collection of principles intended as a guide for behavior and conduct by members of a profession or organization. |
| **Community agencies** | Organizations or entities within communities dedicated to maintaining the common good; including law enforcement, fire departments, paramedics, and comparable emergency responders. |
| **Computer network** | Communications media, devices and software needed to connect two or more computer systems and/or devices. |
| **Confined space** | Compact areas such as tanks, storage bins, hoppers, vaults, pits, sewers, manholes, or any other space with limited openings for entry or exit, unfavorable natural ventilation, or not designed for continuous occupancy but occasionally containing electrical, plumbing, air handling, or other specialized equipment or systems that require some kind of periodic repair or adjustment and requires people to enter such spaces to perform service work. |
| **Conventional office** | Quite high-density regimented row-by-row layout of desks coupled with traditional private offices in which symmetry and uniformity are decisive considera- |

tions; also known as the traditional office layout plan.

**Cost of operation**

Total costs involved with the day-to-day operations of a building or other facility typically including maintenance, repair, administrative, labor, janitorial, house-keeping, utility, cleaning, and related costs.

**Disaster**

A sudden, unplanned, unfortunate disruptive event that results in the potential inability by an organization to perform essential business or operational functions for an undefined period of time.

**Disaster preparedness**

Plans, policies, and procedures developed to ensure that management and personnel are aware of how to respond to potential disasters and how to implement those plans and policies.

**Downsizing**

A reduction in the number of personnel employed in a workforce, reduction in size of organizations, reduction in functions performed within organizations.

**E-business**

A broad definition of electronic commerce that refers not just to buying and selling products but also to servicing customers, collaborating with business partners, and conducting electronic transactions within and among organizations.

**Electrical engineering**

Branch of professional engineering that provides the knowledge, expertise, and specific direction necessary to assure that adequate amounts of electricity will be provided when needed, where needed, and through systems to which requesters for power can connect.

**Electronic mail**
The computer-to-computer exchange of messages, commonly known as "e-mail."

**Electronic records**
Records containing machine-readable information, as opposed to human-readable information, that consists of character-coded electronic signals that can be read and processed through the use of computers.

**Environmental engineering**
Branch of professional engineering that provides the knowledge, expertise, and specific direction necessary to assure that emission control systems, hazardous spill containment, water runoff containment, air quality, and related elements will be appropriately managed.

**Ergonomics**
The science of investigating how worker performance and morale affects physiological and psychological factors in workplaces and the resulting planning of space, technologies, equipment, furniture, and other resources combined with appropriate light, color, sound, and temperature to create high-quality workplace environments.

**Executive champion**
A senior-level executive, top-level government administrator, business owner, senior partner, or other leader in high authority who becomes a strong supporter, proponent and ongoing "champion" of a facilities management program and who works with a facilities manager to advocate, promote and secure support for programs.

**Facilities management**

A profession that encompasses multiple disciplines to ensure functionality of the built environment by integrating people, place, process, technology, and information.

**Facilities management Website**

Website containing online facilities management resources including program descriptions, policies and procedures, program personnel, online processing applications, and related content necessary for and important to the success of facilities management programs.

**Facilities Manager**

Professional individual typically performing wide ranges of leadership functions and with responsibilities for planning, designing, and managing facilities and for coordinating physical workplaces with the people and work of organizations.

**Facilities operations**

The day-to-day activities that involve ongoing operation of electrical systems; heating, ventilating, and air conditioning systems; maintenance procedures; grounds maintenance; and other infrastructure support activities that allow facilities to be operated and used as effectively as possible.

**Facilities plan**

A well-developed comprehensive combination of objectives, goals, strategies, systems, procedures, and processes used as a basis for managing an organization-wide facilities management program.

**Facilities Planning and and Utilization Committee**

Senior-level committee typically including several representatives of an organization's senior management and that functions at a high level within an organization's structure to provide assessments of facilities management needs, prioritization of those needs, and input relative to all aspects of totally integrated workplace development and management.

**Five major elements of organization-wide facilities management programs**

People, information, process, technology, place.

**Furniture**

A variety of components that when combined provide work surfaces, file storage, miscellaneous storage, computer accessories, seating, and other workplace items that serve individual, team, large and small group, special use, and other purposes that benefit occupants within a facility.

**Furniture systems**

Workplaces constructed of components that can be interconnected in widely varying configurations to meet wide varieties of workplace furniture needs.

**Grounds maintenance**

Repairs, maintenance, and other care given to the landscaping, snow removal, and other work related to spaces outside of and surrounding a building structure.

**Hardware**

An IT term relating to the physical equipment used for the input, processing, output and storage activities of a computer system.

**IFMA**

The International Facility Management Association is an international professional association which sponsors and conducts research, provides educational programs, spots and monitors trends, and assists organizational and corporate facilities managers in developing strategies to manage facility, human, and real estate assets (www.ifma.com).

**Implementation**

The process of putting in place a new program or system or converting from one system to another one.

**Information**

Data and facts that are acquired in any way and that are processed into meaningful contexts to become knowledge.

**Intelligent buildings**

Buildings constructed to include computer-based technologies and appropriate communications connections containing sensors that enable monitoring and interacting with building conditions. Maintenance personnel and other building occupants are able to access building management systems consisting of security control, fire control, energy management, environmental and lighting controls, and elevator and escalator controls. Shared occupant services are typically available for voice communications, computer networks, data transmission, and wide varieties of administrative services.

**Integrated workplace design and management**

Processes collectively directed at providing facilities, workstations, manufacturing areas, offices, reception areas, conference rooms, break rooms, training rooms, computer centers, records rooms, corridors or hallways, cafeterias, fitness centers, parking garages, decorative treatments, and other components applied to make those spaces appropriate and pleasant. Workplaces that effectively accommodate and integrate people, information, process, technology, and place.

| | |
|---|---|
| **Interior designers** | Specialists who focus their work on the planning, design, arrangement, configuration, equipping, environmental conditioning, and accenting of efficient, effective, and aesthetically pleasing workplaces. |
| **Internet** | A massive electronic and telecommunications network connecting the computers of many businesses, consumers, government agencies, schools and other organizations, and individuals worldwide. |
| **IT (IS)** | An acronym that typically refers to the unit of organizations that is responsible for organization-wide management of information technology systems functions. IT/IS also refers to any system that collects, processes, stores and analyzes data, and disseminates information for a specific purpose. |
| **Landlord** | Organizations and individuals that own, lease, operate, and manage facilities. |
| **Layout** | A plan created by a facilities manager, space planner, interior designer, office space planner, architect, or other individual showing arrangements and locations of spaces, equipment, furniture, workstations and other common workplace components. |
| **Legal compliance** | The process or procedure to ensure that an organization is following relevant laws and regulations. |
| **Legal requirements** | The obligation under a law to act or not act in a specified manner. |

| | |
|---|---|
| **Lockout/tagout** | Situations in which work on electrical systems requires advance notification and "tagging" to indicate that power supplies have been certifiably shut off (locked out). |
| **Mechanical engineering** | Branch of professional engineering that provides the knowledge, expertise, and specific direction necessary to design, maintain, and manage mechanical equipment of all kinds; usually including heating, cooling, and air handling systems. |
| **Mix of facilities management services** | The variety and scope of facilities management outcomes and services currently being provided by a facilities management department or unit to support client/customer needs and organizations' requirements. |
| **Mobile-aisle file** | Movable file shelves providing high-density file storage that are moved either manually or by motors on tracks placed on floors. |
| **Motivation** | A personal internal process that causes people to take some particular action because they want to take that action. |
| **Office landscaping** | Process of developing open-plan office layouts and designs, an open-plan office layout and design. |
| **Office services** | Miscellaneous services such as mail, copying, reprographics, office supplies, and telecommunications provided for occupants within a building or buildings and that are commonly centralized services shared by all occupants within a facility. |

| | |
|---|---|
| **Open-plan office layout** | Office layout plan which emphasizes the avoidance of sameness and encompasses consideration of work flows, traffic patterns, communication needs, and minimization of privacy and privilege to feature larger open landscapes rather than enclosed or separated areas; often spaces divided by movable partitions. |
| **Open-shelf file** | Side-opening shelf-based file equipment, also referred to as lateral fixed-shelf (non-drawer) file. |
| **Organization** | A functional unit of people, equipment, and facilities that is created, arranged, and integrated with the objective of performing work and operating as a combined entity. |
| **Organization business plan** | A well-developed comprehensive combination of objectives, goals, strategies, systems, procedures, processes, and measurements used as a basis for managing an entity-wide business plan. |
| **Outsourcing** | In a broad sense, the purchase of any product or service from another company, individual, or other entity—such as the purchase of inactive records storage and management from a commercial records storage company. |
| **Place** | Anywhere on earth identifiable through GPS systems or anywhere in the universe that has been charted and mapped; more narrowly, a region, area, location, or spot devoted to a specific purpose. |
| **Preventive maintenance** | Planned steps undertaken to assure and continue appropriate levels of performance by providing repetitively scheduled |

inspections and tasks to prolong the useful life of facilities and systems.

**Process**

A particular method of doing something that generally involves a number of steps or operations performed in a certain or prescribed sequence.

**Project**

An activity that is initiated within Facilities Management or that begins as a direct result of an inquiry from a tenant or potential tenant that is in need of and is soliciting facilities management expertise and assistance.

**Real estate**

Properties, whether they be land and/or building structures, that are necessary and used to provide facilities within which organization's personnel can perform work that contributes to achievement of an organization's goals and objectives.

**Real estate portfolio—owned**

An inventory of properties, whether they be land and/or building structures that are presently owned.

**Real estate portfolio—leased**

An inventory of properties, whether they be land and/or building structures that are owned by another entity and contracted for occupancy and use.

**Record**

The result of recording or preserving information on any media with the intent to preserve information that reflects the position or official business of an organization.

**Records center**

A facility or portion of a facility used for storing and managing business records, typically inactive business records.

| | |
|---|---|
| **Records management** | The professional management of information in the physical form of records from the time records are received or created through their processing, distribution, and use to placement in storage and retrieval systems until either eventual elimination or identification for permanent archival retention. It is the management of information through the life cycle of records. |
| **Records Manager** | An individual, knowledgeable in records management, designated by an organization to manage a records management program. |
| **Records retention period** | The period of time during which records must be maintained by an organization because they are needed for operational, legal, fiscal, historical or other purposes. Records should typically be destroyed after the termination of retention periods. |
| **RFID** | Radio Frequency Identification technology in which small programmable integrated circuits are attached to physical items to enable rapid location and efficient management of those items. |
| **Safety engineers** | Professionals who focus their work on assessments of workplace conditions, identification of existing or potential dangers and unsafe practices, and who prescribe solutions for these situations. |
| **Senior management commitment** | The highest organizational level at which exists an understanding for the importance of successful organization-wide facilities management programs and then exhibits support for those programs by providing human resources |

227

and financial resources necessary to sustain facilities at the lowest practical costs and at the highest possible level of effectiveness.

**Shared tenant services**

Services provided and used within a facility or building that allow tenants to share the costs and benefits of technical services, computing, telecommunications, and other services.

**Space chargeback**

The practice of passing on to building occupants the cost of providing space, utilities, furnishings, maintenance, and other commonly shared amenities provided with an occupied space.

**Space standards**

The effective and efficient allocation of space to individuals and/or operational units based on past, present, and anticipated future utilization practices and often related to job level, equipment requirements, storage requirements, building codes, and other influences that dictate how much space should be consumed by various individual and/or business or other operations.

**Stakeholder component**

An organization or individual with a vested interest in the progress and success of an endeavor and that usually is a source of knowledge, expertise, experience, precedence, and basis typically necessary for success.

**Strategic plan**

A plan that impacts directly on and is critical to the success of an organization's primary objectives, goals, and purposes, typically projecting programs for five to ten years.

**Strategies**

Carefully developed plans or methods used to achieve goals and objectives.

**Suppliers**

Individuals, groups, and organizations that invent, develop, produce, and deliver products and services that enable high-quality work lives and high-quality personal lives.

**Technology**

Any manual, automated, or mental process generally using applied sciences and/or items of some type to transform inputs into products or services.

**Telecommuting**

A variation of work scheduling in which employees work away from traditional settings usually using communication technologies and often working at home.

**Tenant**

Occupant of a facility.

**Utilities**

Resources such as electricity, telephone, natural gas, fuel oil, water, wastewater treatment, telecommunications, and related commodities and services that are necessary to provide support for workers located within an organization's facilities.

**Vital records**

Records that contain information required to continue or re-establish operations in the event of a terrorist act or disaster; records necessary to recreate an organization's legal and financial position, and to preserve the rights of the organization and its customers, employees, shareholders, and other stakeholders.

**Web**

World Wide Web, a portion of the Internet that uses the transport functions of the Internet—via a client/server computer architecture—to handle all types of digital information, including text, hypermedia, graphics and sound.

**Workplace**

A place in which an individual or individuals work.

**Workplace standards**

Guidelines used to design, configure, environmentally condition, and allocate workplace space on organization-wide bases according to established criteria.

**Workstation**

A unit of space composed of furniture elements and technologies within which an individual or individuals perform work.

# About the Authors

## *Daniel A. Brathal*

Daniel A. Brathal, B. A., recently retired from his full-time career following nearly 33 years as an administrative executive at the headquarters of 3M Company in St. Paul, Minnesota. At 3M, his last two assignments were as Manager of Contributions for 3M Community Affairs and as Manager, Strategic Planning and Quality. Prior to those assignments, Mr. Brathal was Manager, 3M Corporate Site Management, 3M Administrative Services, and was responsible for Facilities Management Services, Records Management Services, Forms Management Services, Electronic Document Imaging, Custodial Services, Business Continuity Services, and Administrative Services Systems Support. His 3M facilities management career from 1984 to 1999 included responsibilities for management (planning, design, development, furnishing, maintenance, space allocation, personnel moves, and related functions) of all 3M research and administrative buildings and facilities in St. Paul and the greater Twin Cities area.

Prior to his 3M facilities management positions, Mr. Brathal held positions within 3M as Manager, Corporate Records Management from 1979 to 1984; Supervisor, Micrographic Services from 1974 to 1979; Supervisor, Information Systems Analysis and Design from 1972-1974; and as Records and Office Machine Repair Coordinator from 1970 to 1972.

A U. S. Army veteran of the Viet Nam War, Mr. Brathal worked in administrative operations for the Chicago and Northwestern Railroad after his military service from 1968 until joining 3M in 1970. A native of Baldwin, Wisconsin, he attended the Minnesota School of Business prior to his military service and while an executive at 3M earned a B.A. (Summa Cum Laude) from Concordia University in St. Paul, Minnesota, majoring in Business Administration.

Dan Brathal has been President of the Minneapolis/St. Paul Chapter of the International Facility Management Association (IFMA), was an active leader in the chapter for many years, and earned the chapter's Distinguished Service Award. He was President of the Minnesota Chapter of the Association for Information and Image Management (AIIM) and was

231

selected for induction into the AIIM Company of Fellows. He was President for two terms and held several other leadership positions for the Twin Cities Chapter of ARMA International. The Twin Cities Chapter of ARMA International recognized him as a Chapter Member of the Year.

At 3M, Mr. Brathal was a member, steering committee member, and Chair of the 3M Office Administrative Forum. He was also a member and steering committee member of the 3M Administrative Leadership Symposium, a member of the 3M Technical Council Safety, Health, and Environment Committee, and of the 3M Corporate Records Retention Committee. Mr. Brathal has served his community through his involvement with the Mentoring Partnership of Minnesota and the Minnesota Business Partnership. He has won recognition in *Who's Who in U. S. Executives*.

Daniel A. Brathal is the co-author of three books, has been published in several magazines and professional journals, and he has delivered more than 75 formal presentations at various international and other conferences, conventions, seminars, colleges, and universities throughout the United States and Canada. He is currently President of The Workplace Design Consortium, a facilities design and management consulting organization. Dan and his colleagues specialize in conducting in-depth assessments and analyses of facilities management situations and provide consultations relative to the development and strengthening of organization-wide facilities management programs. Dan Brathal is an effective speaker whose executive briefings on facilities management and content-filled seminars are always highly rated by executives and participants at all levels.

For additional information about Dan's consulting and professional development services, please log on to his website at www.high-performancefacilitiesmanagement.com.

Dan and his wife Jacque live in Hudson, Wisconsin, where they devote many energies and resources to their extended families, their church, their community, their friends, and to each other. Dan continues his active professional career and is committed to making multiple positive differences in the lives of others through his work.

Contact Dan Brathal at 768 Gherty Lane in Hudson, Wisconsin 54016.

# About the Authors

## *Dr. Mark Langemo, CRM*

Dr. Mark Langemo, CRM, is a Professor Emeritus in the College of Business and Public Administration at the University of North Dakota where he was a senior professor from 1972 to 1999. He has over 36 years of experience as a university professor of information systems, records management, office systems management, office layout and design, and related information management courses. Dr. Langemo has been selected as the University of North Dakota's Teacher of the Year and he earned UND's Saiki Award for "excellence in undergraduate instruction."

He received a national award from the University Continuing Education Association for "excellence in continuing education seminars." He has been the executive vice president of a commercial records management company in the Twin Cities of Minneapolis and St. Paul, Minnesota, while on a sabbatical from UND. He was also a long-time member of the Board of Directors of a national bank in North Dakota.

Mark Langemo participates in business and professional development through his records management seminars, consulting, and writing for publication. Known as an enthusiastic and dynamic speaker who presents content-filled, practical, and entertaining records management seminars, he has conducted over 600 seminars spanning 47 of the United States, most Canadian provinces, Australia, Iceland, New Zealand, Trinidad and in Europe.

Dr. Langemo has consulted to the U. S. and Canadian federal governments, state and provincial governments, major corporations such as Microsoft and 3M, city and county governments, energy and power companies, accounting firms, banks, health care organizations, law firms, professional associations, and the John F. Kennedy Space Center in Florida. He is the author or co-author of six books, and he has published over 60 magazine and journal articles.

For additional information about Mark's consulting and professional development services, please log on to his website at www.high-performancefacilitiesmanagement.com.

Mark Langemo earned a BS degree from Valley City State University in 1963 and in 1997 received that university's Distinguished Alumni Award. He earned a MS degree from the University of North Dakota in 1966 and a Doctor of Education (Ed.D.) degree from the University of North Dakota in 1972. In 1979, he received the Certified Records Manager (CRM) designation from the Institute of Certified Records Managers. He was inducted into ARMA International's Company of Fellows in 1991. In 1993, Dr. Langemo received the Emmett Leahy Award from the Institute of Certified Records Managers. The Leahy Award is the highest award internationally in the profession of records and information management.

Mark and his wife Diane live in Grand Forks, North Dakota, spend much of their summers at a Minnesota lake home, and winter at their home in Naples, Florida. He devotes his energies to Diane and her interests, to three sons and their families, to two grandchildren, and to playing both senior softball and senior baseball on the Southwest Florida coast. He continues an active semi-retirement career consulting, conducting records management seminars, writing for publication, and striving to make positive differences in the lives of others.

Contact Mark Langemo at 2534 Sara Lyn Drive in Grand Forks, North Dakota 58201.